STORIES FROM THE STREETS

THERESA MITCHELL
AGAPE OUTREACH INC.

Copyright © Theresa Mitchell

First published in Australia in 2021
by MMH Press
Waikiki, WA 6169

All Rights Reserved. No part of this book may be used or reproduced by any means, graphic, electronic, or mechanical, including photocopying, recording, taping or by any information storage retrieval system without the written permission of the copyright owner except in the case of brief quotations embodied in critical articles and reviews.

Because of the dynamic nature of the Internet, any web addresses or links contained in this book may have changed since publication and may no longer be vaild. The views expressed in this work are solely those of the author and do not necessarily reflect the views of the publisher and the publisher hereby disclaims any responsibility for them.

Edited by Tracey Regan
Cover & interior design by Dylan Ingram & Chelsea Wilcox

A catalogue record for this work is available from the National Library of Australia

National Library of Australia Catalogue-in-Publication data:
Stories from the Streets/Theresa Mitchell

ISBN: 978-0-6451484-5-9
(Paperback)

ISBN: 978-0-6451484-6-6
(eBook)

If you see a person in need, help them.
It is that easy.
-Theresa Mitchell

CONTENTS

Foreword 1
Government regulations 3
Who is Homeless? 11
What Causes Homelessness? 15
Youth Homelessness 25
Homeless Pets 27
Unconditional Love 28
1. Theresa 33
2. Anon 35
3. Anon 37
4. Ryan 38
5. Anon 40
6. Anon 43
7. Judgement 45
8. Falling through the cracks 49
9. George 53
10. Trigger Warning 54
11. Anon 57
12. John 59

13. Mr Rentals	61
14. Tim	62
15. Tara	65
16. Anon	67
17. Beyond Yourself	71
18. Max	73
19. Ronnie	75
20. Gayle	79
21. Carol	80
22. Jacob	83
23. Anon	86
24. Eve	88
25. Ruckus	91
26. Anon	97
27. Homelessness - a price to pay	105
28. David	109
29. Faye's Story	110
30. Melissa Groom	115
Agape's Dream Tiny Housing Living Estates	123
Theresa Mitchell	126

FOREWORD

Have you ever wondered how a homeless person became that way? What happened in their life to bring them to this place of poverty? Is it mental illness, drugs or has the person been through something gut-wrenchingly terrible? Stories from the Streets will help you find the answers for yourself.

The following stories are an accumulation of real-life events, their experience of being homeless, and the impact this has had on their lives.

The stories have been compiled from interactions with clients within the charity: Agape Outreach Inc. based in Tweed Heads, Australia. They include submitted life stories from the people connected with Agape, either as direct clients, or through connected Domestic Violence refuges, or from some of our volunteers who have chosen to give back after turning their lives around.

Some of the stories have been written as a small snapshot of a person's life or as an overview of major events as told to Agape's founder, Theresa Mitchell. In some cases, names have been changed or omitted to protect an individual's privacy and a generic photo may have been used.

THERESA MITCHELL

Agape Outreach Inc. is a service that provides meals to those who are hungry on the streets of the Gold Coast QLD, Tweed Heads and Byron Shire NSW.

Agape also provides free, person-centred support, psychologist appointments, life coaching, life skills training, and drug and/or alcohol support programs, as well as case management to assist with applying for housing or access to showers and laundry services.

Agape is actively working towards the goal of 'tiny' housing estates. These will be supported living estates for the homeless and needy, situated nationally around Australia, and will provide permanent housing as well as daily support for the chronic homeless, as needed. Agape is seeking corporate sponsorship to help make this dream a reality.

For more information on Agape Outreach Inc. please connect with us at www.agapeoutreachinc.com or find us on Facebook, Instagram or Twitter.

GOVERNMENT REGULATIONS

The Australian Federal Government has a lack of policies in place for dealing with homelessness, which leaves many local governments naïve to the complex needs of the disenfranchised. Some states respond well for the benefit of the people, while others push the boundaries of unethical conduct and pass the blame onto the Federal Government. *However, how we treat people in our community should be everyone's problem.*

The United Nations, 'International Covenant on Economic, Social and Cultural Rights' under Article 11, provides a full and detailed description of human rights relating to food, water and shelter. We are unable to provide the full description due to copyright laws, but we have summarised the points below:

1 Everyone has a right to an 'adequate' standard of living conditions including clothing, food and shelter.

2 Food - Dependent upon economic and other conditions, present and future generations are entitled to food security.

3 Water - Everyone is entitled to access a safe water source for domestic or personal use.

4 Housing - Adequate shelter means a place of privacy and

security, with safe drinking water, sanitation and access to energy for cooking etc.

Can the right to an adequate standard of living be limited?

Measures that are retrogressive to the realisation of economic, social and cultural rights must also be ***properly justified***. A retrogressive measure is one that reduces the extent to which an economic, social and cultural right is guaranteed.[1]

In December 2019, the local member for Coolangatta, cancelled all permits for charities to hand out food to the disenfranchised in parks, saying that, 'Food provision enables people to stay homeless and that handing out clothing or a blanket to a homeless person is a domestic activity that belongs in a house, not on public land.'

Our response; a person going without a meal does not make housing magically appear for them, and giving them a meal does not make them choose to stay homeless, but it does show them that someone cares and is willing to help. It gives them someone to trust who may be able to help find housing when they are ready.

Food, clothing and blankets may belong in a house but so do people, please provide one for them.

Keep in mind that organisations like Agape are not funded by government, and forcing us out of public areas into paid halls risks our organisation's closure from financial stress. The local members could be assisting to solve the problem by helping us to gain access to buildings, more housing and reducing

---

[1] Cited on the 21/02/1021 *from* **https://www.ag.gov.au/rights-and-protections/human-rights-and-anti-discrimination/human-rights-scrutiny/public-sector-guidance-sheets/right-adequate-standard-living-including-food-water-and-housing#what-is-the-right-to-an-adequate-standard-of-living**

homeless numbers with compassion. In the meantime vulnerable people are dying in the elements, while the local members continue to deny there is a problem.

Homeless charity Agape Outreach says it's been forced out of Public Park by Gold Coast Council just a week out from Christmas
ABC Gold Coast / By Dominic Cansdale
Posted Monday 23 December 2019 at 6:21am: Agape Outreach has provided free food to homeless people in Goodwin Park, Coolangatta, for more than 10 years. *(Supplied: Agape Outreach)*

Key points:
- City of Gold Coast says 'additional services' such as free clothing and laundry are no longer allowed in council parks
- Homeless charity Agape Outreach has operated in Goodwin Park in Coolangatta for more than a decade
- The charity says it will struggle to find a nearby private venue to replace the park

THERESA MITCHELL

Agape Outreach organises free food, laundry, clothing and veterinary services along the Byron, Tweed and Gold Coast, and has used Goodwin Park in Coolangatta for more than a decade.

Founding director Theresa Mitchell said council officers informed her just over a week ago that her charity's services were 'no longer acceptable in their parks.'

'Full stop it's low. It's even lower at Christmas,' Ms Mitchell said.

'We've had our permit cancelled a few times and I understand that when people start to make complaints, they [the council] have asked us to move to another area.

'But this is the first time council has actually turned around and said 'you're not welcome here on any of our properties'.'

Huge demand from homeless but nowhere to go

Agape Outreach feeds around 80 people a night, twice a week in Goodwin Park but now has until mid-January 2020 to find a private venue within walking distance.

'Council has declared all these things as domestic duties that belong in a house and are no longer available or allowed in their parks,' Ms Mitchell said.

'When we first started 10 years ago we were getting 25 and that has now increased to an average of 80 people a night.'

But Ms Mitchell said recently a group of three homeless people with substance abuse issues had caused problems.

STORIES FROM THE STREETS

Agape Outreach operates along the Byron, Tweed and Gold Coast. *(Supplied: Agape Outreach)*

She said her efforts to address this with local authorities several months ago went unheard.

'They don't have an understanding of homelessness or addiction,' she said.

'Their decision on those three people affects 80 people.'

Gold Coast council defends decision

A spokesperson for the City of Gold Coast said in a statement that council 'does not want to cancel all regular meal services' but wants to reduce their regularity and remove additional services like clothing and laundry.

'It is the responsibility of the City to manage City parks to ensure that all users have a safe and enjoyable park experience,' the spokesperson said.

'Safety concerns have been raised by City officers, welfare groups, and members of the public regarding the behaviour of some of the event attendees.

'The City continues to work very closely with the Department of Housing and Public Works, Queensland Health, Specialist Homeless Services, and the Queensland Police Service to ensure the safety and welfare of all Gold Coast residents.'

Agape Outreach held its 10th annual Christmas Party at Goodwin Park on December 11. *(Supplied: Agape Outreach)*

But Ms Mitchell said the council's attitude towards homeless people was out of touch.

'Homeless people aren't one classification,' she said.

'I've got people down there with cancer, I've got families, I've even got senior citizens who can't afford to eat once they pay their rent.

'They don't need more trauma. They need someone to care for them.'

STORIES FROM THE STREETS

Attitudes toward homeless a broader problem

Earlier this month, 420 people attended Agape Outreach's 10th annual Christmas event at Goodwin Park.

She said her charity had grown over the years to help homeless and needy people across the coast, and that affordable housing was not keeping up with demand.

'Housing is in such short supply, it is really hard for someone to get into these places,' Ms Mitchell said.

'You might have eighty applicants per house.'

Ms Mitchell said she will struggle to find a new private venue big enough and cheap enough to house her large clientele.

'To hire a hall to feed eighty-plus people in, they're in limited supply,' she said.

'We're not going to get into community centres that are government-run anyway, so parks really have the biggest space for us.'

In 2020, during COVID-19, Southport and Surfers Paradise started to enforce similar rules against charities who support the disenfranchised. The council employed rangers to travel between Coolangatta and the northern Gold Coast to continually move on homeless people.

Fines have been imposed, not just for the homeless, but for anyone handing a meal out to a person on the street. Agape has had rangers threaten $640 fines per person, for handing a meal to someone without food.

Gold Coast council says it is a violation of Law 9 to aid a person in need on public land and anyone can be fined $640 for doing so. (Law 9 is linked below but we have been unable to identify a direct violation listed in the law for giving a person food. The violation is for unpermitted use of a public space and GC council cancelled the permits.)

https://www.goldcoast.qld.gov.au/documents/ll/ll-9-pks-reserves-consolidated.pdf

Other regular practices of the council are to lock the public toilets overnight, in order to stop the homeless sleeping in them, and also turning off water and barbeques in the parks.

How does this fit in with 'The International Covenant on Economic, Social and Cultural Rights,' that everyone should have sustainable access to natural and common resources, safe drinking water, energy for cooking, heating and lighting, sanitation and washing facilities, means of food storage, refuse disposal, site drainage and emergency services?

Our expectation is not that local government should have an answer to fixing the homelessness problem, but don't disadvantage people by removing their access to items that are basic rights. Perhaps, consultation with non-funded organisations who are working directly on the streets with the homeless, would be a step towards understanding the problems of homelessness in the community.

It's very easy to point a finger and say, 'Look, they defecate in the park,' but when sanitary facilities are locked, the outcome wouldn't be different for you or me.

WHO IS HOMELESS?

When asking people in the community what they believe homelessness is, a common response is; dole bludgers and addicts. 'Why don't they just get a job?' Yet, when asked to visually describe a homeless person, the description is of an old man (probably with mental illness), with matted hair pushing around his life possessions in a shopping trolley.

Most people don't understand that homelessness affects people like you and me; families, the elderly, children and many more. Both the first mentioned scenarios are a part of homelessness, but these are only the most visual representation of the cohort, and if we tell ourselves that they choose this lifestyle, then we don't need to do anything! Putting our head in the sand won't make the problem go away.

To the contrary, homelessness is growing. COVID-19 is seeing more and more families pushed into homelessness and the coming few years will be dark times for many. Community reports are indicating that families paying rent of up to $800 per week are struggling to find new accommodation and the same effects are impacting the purchasing of houses. With so many applicants, houses are selling up to $100k above asking price within a couple of hours of being on the market. Some people are saying that they have applied to rent up to 80 houses unsuccessfully.

Homeless people are just people like you and me. They are people who have experienced trauma which has continued to impact their lives until the situation becomes uncontrollable. When we understand this, we are more ready to show compassion and support.

While many people have a heart and want to help, as a country we are yet to recognise the mammoth need for change on a national level.

Unfortunately the nature of homelessness is isolation and hiding, often due to feelings of shame. With some of the homeless, not even their own families see the full extent of how devastating, life-changing and dangerous their situation has become. Statistics are usually understated because of the shame that surrounds being homeless. Many homeless people keep themselves hidden away.

When working with a person on the streets, I will always try to obtain some family information in case of an emergency. More often than not, the person is reluctant to offer it, as their children and loved ones, in most cases, are not aware that they are homeless or in financial trouble.

Many families don't learn of the struggles of their loved ones until it is too late to assist them. The depression and hopelessness of being on the street, drives many people to substance abuse in a bid to help them cope. Over time, mental illness takes over.

The stigma associated with homelessness holds some family members back from helping their loved ones, resulting in some cases, with the disenfranchised being shunned by the people they care for.

STORIES FROM THE STREETS

Shame can stop people from asking for help and also from giving it. How sad it is to let a feeling like shame determine an individual's quality of life.

Homeless people are:
- Fathers & Mother
- Sisters & Brothers
- Sons & Daughters
- Aunts & Uncles
- Teenagers
- Babies & children
- Grandparents
- Families
- Senior citizens

Homelessness does not discriminate; no one is immune.

Almost all people who are experiencing homelessness are going through some kind of trauma; loss, grief, accident, ill health, domestic violence, family violence, financial trauma. Any life situation that stops a person from being able to function normally within mainstream living, has the potential to leave them homeless and living on the streets. The risk is far greater if the person has no family support network. We are all one trauma away from homelessness.

As homeless people look just like you and I, chances are you are walking past the homeless every day and are not even aware of it.

Stop and think for a minute.

Have you ever been in a situation, even momentarily, of wondering around the streets with nowhere to go, nowhere to turn and asking yourself, 'What do I do now?'

> While I have never had to personally sleep rough, I have found myself in a new town, not knowing anyone and having my drug addict boyfriend throw me out the house with only the clothes on my back.
>
> No matter how momentary the time is, it is an awful feeling and the mental complexity of not knowing what to do or where to go brings up gut-wrenching anxiety and helplesness.
>
> -*Theresa Mitchell*

This brief experience enlightened my awareness of what others are going through, while it may be invisible in our exterior shell.

We walk around every day, busy with work, errands and thoughts of our future plans, completely oblivious if the person we just walked past may be wondering if it will be days before they eat again, or where they can hide from their partner's violence.

WHAT CAUSES HOMELESSNESS?

In short, anyone who goes through a debilitating trauma and has minimal support around them is likely to become homeless. The death of a loved one, a bad divorce, a bad accident, serious health issues, family or domestic violence, housing shortages and financial trauma, can all cause homelessness.

> 'The largest **cause of homelessness** is **Domestic Violence.**'
> - *Mission Australia.*

Domestic violence pushes both men and women into homelessness when all other options are unavailable.

A couple of years ago, domestic violence (DV) was a national focus and many DV refuges were opened. Since then funding cuts and strict council legislations have seen many of those DV refuges closed. Finding a bed can take time to organise and a person may have to move across states to be housed or more likely, they remain homeless having to sleep rough.

While priorities are made for women with children, we still see a shortage of both temporary and permanent housing, including refuges. This results in growing numbers of families living in their vehicles, sleeping in tents or paying their whole income into a motel just to keep a roof over their head. Agape has had families paying $800 per week for a motel room to live in, and the family has no money for food, petrol, school uniforms or any way to change their circumstances.

We are in great need of more DV refuges, including those that cater for pets. Some perpetrators threaten and harm pets in an attempt to control their victims, and many women won't leave their situation unless they can take their pet with them.

Another crack in the system of refuges, is that older teenage boys are not allowed into a refuge for fear they will be violent like their fathers. The reality is, women can only enter a refuge if they leave their pets and teenage sons with the perpetrator (assuming there is no other safe place).

Woman with children, young families and low income earners find themselves homeless with consistently rising rental prices and increasing costs of living. This can force low-income families onto the streets, living in cars or motels. Along with a lack of housing, finding a desired rental that is affordable is becoming like winning the lottery.

> Statistics show that the majority of people are just two pay weeks away from homelessness.

Housing department housing

The waiting list for housing in some cases, can be up to twenty years. With each suburban area receiving as few as nine houses per year from the local government (as Tweed Heads does), the wait time doesn't get any shorter.

Other complexities are that some young families will not seek help from services after becoming homeless because of fear that Family Services will take away their children. This is a genuine concern for many young families and places massive pressure on families. As stated previously, we see many paying their whole income into a motel room just to ensure their children will stay with them.

Agape Outreach Inc. helps many young families in these circumstances with food and sometimes school transport for the kids.

> 'The Australian Bureau of Statistics and Australian Institute of Health and Welfare report that families with children are the fastest growing group of Australians experiencing homelessness (an increase of 17% between 2001 and 2006) represent a quarter of the total homeless population. These figures indicate that ONE IN THREE HOMELESS IS A CHILD.'
> – *Dr Ruth Knight, Zark Consultancy:*
> ***www.zarkconsultancy.com*** *Life house project*

> The 2016 census told us that older women, those aged 55 and above, are now the fastest growing cohort within Australian homelessness, increasing by 31%. The ongoing shortage of affordable housing and the significant gap in financial inequality between men and women suggests this trend may continue.
> – *The Human Rights Commission*

As we approach the 2021 census, I expect that families may, once again, top the charts in homelessness as the COVID-19 pandemic has hit the tourism trade the hardest in Australia. This means that primarily younger people, casuals and restaurant business owners, many of whom have young families, have been greatly impacted financially.

The coming census will show that despite the government opening up more short-term accommodation to get people off the street during the pandemic, homelessness is still rising. Separate to homelessness, food insecurity and 'at risk of homelessness' figures will be astronomical; people may be living in a home, but can't afford food.

Mental illness

Australia has limited support facilities for the mentally ill.

The mental illness ward in a hospital may take you in for a few months, but after receiving treatment, people are straight back on the streets again, regardless of the need for ongoing treatment.

To have someone institutionalised full-time is a huge process. This is when a person is declared unfit to care for themselves, in any form. It is not for people who still have the ability to function independently in some way. In twelve years of working with Agape, I have only seen two people become institutionalised, as they were unable to feed or toilet themselves.

The other option for people to get off the streets quickly is imprisonment. This means they must commit a crime to get help. For some people who can be violent with their mental illness, sadly they do the rotating cycle of court case after court case, where they hurt someone, go to prison and then they are back out on the street again. This continues until their crime is heinous enough to send them away long-term. People with mental illness need more support than the option of street life versus incarceration. This only fills the jails and doesn't help anyone to have a quality of life.

Many people on the street find jail to be a place where they can have a roof over their head, regular food and somewhere with appropriate boundaries that they may have never experienced before.

STORIES FROM THE STREETS

A few years ago, one of our most lovable personalities on the streets, who wouldn't hurt a fly, ended up locked up for a period of time. I came across him after just being released. He was drunk as a skunk and heading to do some shoplifting.

I asked him to sit and talk with me for a while. It turned out that he was a foster child who had been moved multiple times in his childhood. Moving from home to home repeatedly left him feeling disconnected, unloved and distrusting towards anyone that could be considered 'family.' So, at thirty-five, he was homeless and a chronic alcoholic, drinking to hide his feelings of being rejected.

While he was incarcerated, he was able to sober up. He was given a role in the kitchen cooking, and there were boundaries that stopped him from sabotaging himself. He had never felt as safe as he did in prison. He told me that he was heading off to shoplift again, so he could go back to jail.

The unseen benefit of time in prison was that he gained a healthy normality, a place where he fitted in, a purpose for life, HOPE and boundaries which helped him to see a future. Sadly he never found 'normal' life outside of jail time.

Homelessness for many people originates from a major life trauma, and the inability to function normally post-trauma. Homelessness then impacts greatly on a person's mental health. Chronic sleep deprivation, food insecurity and the hopelessness of the situation result in depression and anxiety, which if left unchecked, can develop into psychotic disorders like schizophrenia. Each of these stages limits a person's ability to function on a socially acceptable level.

Some of society have the expectation that the homeless

need to get a job and move on into mainstream living, but this is far from the reality for many people. The longer a person has been living on the street, the deeper the depression or mental illness. For some, it has been decades since living in any form of 'normal' lifestyle, and turning this around in anything short of years is just not possible. If we want to change homelessness, then let's change our expectations to a person-centred level that supports the individual's abilities and immediate needs.

Mental illness stops people from being able to claim **welfare payments**. If you can't sit for intensive interviews, fill in paperwork and follow the ongoing instructions to keep a payment, well, you can't have a payment. And having a disability doesn't necessarily entitle you to a disability pension. Many homeless receive no government support and would be surviving out of trash cans if not for the free meal services which are mostly run by the community and not-for-profit organisations.

We have worked with war veterans on the street that are unable to go inside buildings without reacting in terror and needing to be in the open so they can feel safe. Women who have been physically abused can get to the point where something snaps in their mind. They live permanently in a place of denial, believing that they are loved and housed with a family, but in reality, they are sleeping under bushes and eating out of bins. This even stops them from accepting help.

Homelessness has never fit into a box, so why do we have policies that only help people that tick the 'correct' boxes.

If you don't get a government payment, you can't access free healthcare, you can't go on the list for housing and people already in housing department houses are not allowed anyone else to stay with them. If they allow others to stay, they are at risk of losing their house.

> 58% of the homeless population are male and 42% are female. Over 116,000 people were homeless in Australia according to the 2016 census.
> – *https://www.homelessnessaustralia.org.au/about/homelessness-statistics*

While no figures have been recorded since then, the number of people who are homeless has greatly increased over the last few years and the forecast is that the number will quadruple over the next two decades, with senior citizen women becoming one of the highest figures.

Senior citizens are fast becoming one of the highest figures of homelessness in Australia. We are working with many older Australians who are unable to afford the high cost of living. As a matter of interest, it is more affordable to live in Melbourne than on the Gold Coast; this is taken from the ratio of income versus rent affordability.

We are seeing increasing numbers of senior women who have been widowed, with their stepchildren evicting them from their homes, leaving them homeless or in financial insecurity, unable to pay bills.

The **Aussie swaggie,** while in the minority, is alive and well. Some of our swaggies have been on the streets for forty years and are not a problem to anyone. They travel up and down the coast going to the warmth of the north for the winter and moving south in the summer. They have no addictions; they keep themselves clean, dress well and keep to themselves. This is a lifestyle they are attracted to and will always live. At Agape, we estimate that as little as 2% of homeless people (2 out of 100) choose to live this way, as opposed to the other 98% who are homeless due to lack of options.

I'm sure you've heard stories of people living in a tent or shelter, and when they passed away it was discovered they had millions of dollars in the bank. These people are usually our 'swaggies.'

Addiction: Street life causes addiction

People dealing with emotional trauma often resort to substance use. While addiction is not isolated to people experiencing past or present trauma, this demographic is representative of a high number of people experiencing addiction and homelessness.

Large numbers of homeless people come from a childhood of living in care. Some have moved homes over thirty times during their childhood, which averages at around three months at a time with each family. The burning hole within them for love screams out, but fear pushes them away in an attempt to protect themselves, because history tells them that those they care about will be gone from their lives again soon. This emotional hole is often filled with alcohol, drugs and sometimes violence.

There is a lack of research into the statistics of whether substance abuse causes homelessness or homelessness triggers substance use. The most plausible answer is both. Some people with high substance use lose their homes and the hopelessness, along with constant fear and high anxiety, pushes people to seek to numb the pain.

A study on the homeless in London found that 80% of substance using participants reported starting using a substance after becoming homeless. Fountain, Howes, Marsden, et al. (2003) Drug and alcohol use and the link with homelessness: Results from a survey of homeless people in London. Addiction Research and Theory, 11(4):245-256.

The relationship between high substance use and trauma needs to be researched, as studies would benefit greatly if a correlation between trauma and homelessness was found, while viewing substances as a side effect of the main cause.

Sadly, those with substance problems and mental illness are the least supported cohorts within poverty, while being the highest at risk. We must find a way to intervene and provide preventative measures, to stop either classification causing the other.

Photo credit to Shaun Lister

Glimpse of Agape Outreach 2020

Agape Means; self-sacrificial love, the same love that Jesus showed by dying on the cross for us.

Overview as at 17/12/20	2019	2020	% +/-
Volunteers	100	150	+50%
Hot meals	9640	14700	+52.5%
Food hampers	8000	8580	+7.25%
Case management	83	460	+434.8%
Rescued food	83 tonnes	63 tonnes	-31.74%

- Agape turned 11 years old on Australia Day on January 2, 2020 we are nearly 12 years old
- We have over 150 volunteers now, they live from New Zealand to Sydney to Brisbane
- Our new mobile meal service covering Byron Bay NSW to Runaway Bay Qld has provided over 14,700 free hot meals (which is a 52.5% increase from last year!!!), fresh produce, clothing and other essentials, available to anyone in need and has been running 11 years and 11 months
- Assistance with food hamper support to over 8,580 people which has increased significantly this year due to COVID
- We have provided clothing and furniture items in homes for 111 people in need to the value of $1966 in our shop alone, not counting the thousands of items handed out on the streets
- Case Management have assisted over 460 people needing to move forward with housing and other serious needs this is up 434.8% from 83 people in 2019 when there were only 2 people were doing case management
- Agape rescued over 63 tonnes of food this year that was given back to people in need, both in precooked meals and food hampers this amount feel due to food shortages with COVID
- Life coaching for emotional support turned into the opening of Agape's own psychology department and the commencement of drug and alcohol programs.

A huge thank you for your support this year – Wishing you many blessings from everyone at AGAPE

YOUTH HOMELESSNESS

Unsafe, violent home environments are the main cause for **youth homelessness.** Youth are not necessarily visible on the streets because they are more likely to couch surf and be transient, moving around from place to place. Because of the transient nature, it is harder to record reliable statistics. It is likely that the numbers of homeless youth are far higher than represented.

> On any night in Australia over 44,000 youth under twenty-four years of age are homeless, with close to 18,000 OF THOSE BEING UNDER TWELVE YEARS OLD.
> – *https://www.aihw.gov.au/reports/children-youth/australias-children/contents/housing/homelessness*
> The major cause of youth homelessness is family conflict and breakdown.

Photo credit to Shaun Lister

HOMELESS PETS

Pets are common among the homeless and the love between them is often closer than the person has had with any other human being.

The pet becomes their main companion, a comfort providing unconditional love. They are a form of safety and fill the hole of loneliness for those on the streets. Pets are warmth to lay beside on a cold night, and loyal, way beyond how many people act.

Basically, a pet for a homeless person can be everything to them.

We often find that our clients will go without meals to feed their dog or cat. While the animal may not always receive the best that life has to offer, there is no doubt they are loved and that they mean the world to their owners.

Agape has donated animal food for pets. We also have a volunteer vet within our organisation who looks after the animals. Currently we are looking for a mobile dog wash to partner with us and bless these wonderful fur babies.

Some people look at the homeless and their pets and judge that it's not right to have pet if you don't have a home. But isn't everyone entitled to be loved?

Thankfully more people are realising their pets can be a lifeline for the homeless, and most of their animals are treated better than they treat themselves.

UNCONDITIONAL LOVE

When we place any expectation on our giving, we make our expression of love conditional. We also place ourselves at risk of hardening our hearts to others in need.

While we may be able to justify hardening our hearts in certain circumstances, keep in mind that it is us, our heart, that we are changing. This may make us feel safer but at the same time we are hanging on to pain which hurts us in the long run.

Are you a giving person or a person who gives only when the recipient seems worthy of our blessing? Honestly, do some introspection here and see what the answer is. If you are a giving person then give because that is who you are. Let the boundaries of giving be based on your wealth and time to give, not on the expectation or reason for giving. If you are in a position to give then become an active giver.

There is always someone who will try to take everything on offer, but don't let that person stop you from helping others. It's more important that we be true to who we are as a person than let someone steal our goodness.

Set appropriate boundaries around giving. If you can't afford to give without it ever being returned, don't give it! Many people give with the expectation that it will be returned and then they hold grudges, sometimes for the rest of their lives, because it wasn't. If we expect it back it really wasn't a gift. Life will be much freer if the expectation of returning money is removed. Pivot your thoughts around to giving freely without any attachment. If anything is returned you have received a blessing, but don't expect it.

Our expectation of thanks can dampen our desire to give if our expectations are not met. What would happen if we were to change our expectation? People often don't respond in a manner that we would like them to. A person with depression is more likely to show no emotion than a heartfelt thank you. Their response doesn't change their need, or even their appreciation, so please don't let it change your core foundation for being a giver.

Remember that giving isn't just about money. We all have something to give; an ear to listen, a lift when needed, mowing the neighbour's nature strip or babysitting to give weary parents time out. The bottom line is, if you don't have it to give, you can't afford to lose it, so don't give it. When you do give, don't expect it back. If it does comes back then it's a wonderful bonus.

Many people believe in karma and that it works in immediate or controllable blessings. Do you believe if you bless someone, it will be returned next week when you put in your lotto ticket? Or if you fall on hard times, do you resent the blessings that are not returned to you? If so, then that is not unconditional.

Doors will open and people do bless us back over time, but we need to keep a check on ourselves as giving people, that we are not giving with conditions and expectations in mind.

THERESA MITCHELL

> If love is missing in the world, become the love. We have a choice to be a part of the pain or to be a part of the answer.
> *-Theresa Mitchell*

We had a single mother with six kids coming down to our outreach for meals. She had some substance issues and was not always making the best choices for her children.

Some of my volunteers wanted to refuse her help as they felt we were enabling her addiction. I asked them two questions:

1 If we stop feeding the family will she stop using?

2 If we stop providing food for the family, who will feed and be a positive influence for the kids?

Their time at our outreach may have been the only time someone was prepared to invest love into the family, particularly the children. We could easily see that love was greatly needed, so why turn them away?

Agape provides food and support unconditionally. Whether the kids should be in her care or not, is up to the organisations that are funded to deal with these decisions. Agape's role in their lives is small, but I believe it's very important to make the most of every opportunity to show love to people when we have the chance.

If this was my child in this situation, my prayer would be for people to show them love and positive guidance. There is enough judgement in the world and I choose to contribute to being a part of the answer and not the problem.

There are many elderly men that attend our meal program and some of them are in housing department homes, have a pension and no addictions.

STORIES FROM THE STREETS

I encourage them to attend because I know that social isolation causes depression and this is the cause of the highest rate of suicide in men over forty.

While working with many older males who live alone, I regularly see malnutrition, with some eating just a packet of biscuits per day. They slowly decline in body and mental health for lack of nutrition and human interaction.

The Agape program is there to give a sense of belonging, combat social isolation and offer a nutritious meal. Food is a necessity for life, but belonging gives a reason to live that life.

These gentlemen also become the first to step up and help out when we are short on volunteers. They are the most dedicated volunteers available.

Photo credit to Shaun Lister

1. THERESA

> *When my husband left me at three weeks pregnant, in debt and with nothing, I felt*
> *INVISIBLE........................*

After a short six months of marriage, my husband left me when I was three weeks pregnant. I became too sick to work and was thousands in debt. He used the legal system to intimidate me and had his friends call with death threats.

Lack of finance and no local support network meant the entire amount of my social security payment went into rent and I could only pay just enough to keep the electricity connected. A phone line was unaffordable.

I couldn't afford food, so I lived off fruit and bread given to me by a friend, and the free morning tea at church on Sunday. Some weeks I would go five days without food.

After my son was born, I searched for charities to get help with food and furniture, but the most I received was a $30 food voucher every other month. With that, I bought formula for my son, as I was unable to feed him due to my stress and lack of nutrition.

I felt invisible and alone.

THERESA MITCHELL

I believe people should never have to walk alone in times of great need.

This is a part of my story and twelve years ago Agape Outreach Inc. serving the homeless and needy was born.

Agape desires to give hope and to help people back to their true purpose. No one can stop bad circumstances from happening in life, but we can walk with people through them.

There have been, and will continue to be, many learning curves from unexpected happenings, but all are character building and help us to develop a set of skills for resilience. Who I have become empowers me to say that I am a better person for the hardships I have endured.

2. ANON

A client with alcohol issues came to our program for a meal, for the second night in a row. We served him his dinner and he sat down. The next thing we knew, he had slumped down onto the table and collapsed. He was unresponsive and cold.

Immediately we moved him into the recovery position and called '000.' The emergency service operator thought he may have had a heart attack, and sent a helicopter as well as an ambulance to support him and get him to hospital quickly. The support sent by the emergency services could not be faulted; we were very impressed, especially that they had sent a helicopter.

After Agape's meal service, I visited the hospital to check on him. They told me that the years of alcohol abuse to his body had severely damaged the organs in his body.

He had attended our meal service the night before and had got wet from a sprinkle of rain. That night he was sleeping on the balcony at his mate's house. He was happy to stay there, as there had recently been a high amount of violence in the area. The temperature that night dropped to 4°C and by the time he had come back to us the following evening, his body had started to shut down. He literally had been dying in front of us.

When he left, the hospital gave him advice that as his organ linings where so thin, if he were to sustain a punch to the stomach or another night in the cold, he would not survive.

He is now in housing, alive and well. If he had collapsed anywhere else without people around him, he would have died that night.

This event became the catalyst for us seeking triple the number of donated blankets over winter. Up until that year, at least one homeless person per year had died in our area from exposure to the elements. We haven't had another death within our circles since then that has been directly related to outdoor exposure.

Working long-term with the homeless teaches us about the people we are, especially around judgement and acceptance. If we are truthful, we can all recognise that we are guilty, in some way, of judgement and lack of acceptance.

3. ANON

During the early days of Agape I started fostering children. I was fostering a child whose parents had significant emotional abuse issues. On multiple nights, I would be left waiting a significant amount of time for the child to be dropped off. One particular night, this behaviour made me late for the street program where I was expected to be, and I inappropriately complained about my annoyance with the child's parents.

It took about three minutes for a lady to walk up to me with tears in her eyes. She told me that her children had been taken away from her and she hadn't seen them in years.

Talk about a frog in the throat. The pain in her eyes was so deep, I felt completely devastated for her and realised I had no right to complain. I was out of line.

That night, I learnt that no matter how incapable a parent is with their children, it doesn't mean they don't love them.

I had seen the pain from both sides of the story and knew that I could no longer assume judgement from either side. There are evil actions in this world but it doesn't mean that a person is evil.

4. RYAN

Ryan rang me one morning, stressed out and completely agitated. After hearing what was going on, he gave me an address. So I grabbed some food and went around.

Ryan had been living homeless under a bridge when social services contacted him to say his ex-partner had handed over their four-year-old autistic son, and because of her mental health issues, she had walked away.

Ryan was told that if he could get permanent housing, he could gain custody of his son. Is it any wonder he was stressed out? He had gone from being homeless into the responsibility of looking after his son and a house full-time.

Housing services had helped by placing him and his young son, Kasey, into temporary housing for eight weeks. They were going to help him find a unit and pay the bond, but somehow he still needed to save two weeks rent in advance, as well as clothe and feed them both. On top of that, he would need to find suitable furniture before moving in to the new accommodation.

Agape provided food, clothes, toys and lots of encouragement for the eight-week temporary housing period, in order to maximise Ryan's chances of him saving the rent he needed in advance, which he did.

STORIES FROM THE STREETS

When it came time to move, kind people in the community donated through us a fridge (which we filled with food), all the kitchenware, beds and bed linen, a lounge, TV, clothes and toys. We even received Christmas presents for Kasey, which Ryan could put away in the cupboard for Christmas the following month.

On our last trip to drop off the furniture, Kasey took my little finger and led me from room to room showing me all the new furniture and the soft, comfy pillows. He was so excited for their new home.

Moments like this with Kasey are the reason we do what we do.

5. ANON

Before I became homeless I was a counsellor and had spent eight-and-a-half years at university and two years at TAFE. I guess you could say I am an educated woman. I also have mental health issues (depression, anxiety and PTSD), and was suicidal.

Having recently moved to country NSW from the City, I struggled to find work, and without employment was unable to sustain my rental house.

My mental health issues got progressively worse, and as my savings dwindled, the realisation hit me that my cat and I were about to be homeless for the first time. The last of my savings were spent on urgent dental work (not covered by the public dental system) and then I put my cat in a cattery and my belongings into storage. Needless to say there was no money left to accommodate myself.

I rang a crisis line, but they could only offer a few nights in cheap motels and after that, when I refused the caravan park from hell, I was on my own. All dignity was gone when I then had to live on the streets, as there were no homeless shelters for single, mature women.

I decided to camp on a park bench between the police station and the courthouse as I felt safer there. It was well-lit and

STORIES FROM THE STREETS

I had twenty-four-hour access to the bathroom at the police station. I lost a lot of weight as there wasn't much to eat without a fridge and being vegan, and I felt the hope quickly drain from me, as no one was able to help.

Filling in the days without endlessly loitering was challenging and I found it convenient to spend the days at the community centre where I could occasionally have a hot shower, as it was cold after only a few uses. I could do my washing there, eat and drink, and feel safe. Weekends were the worst, as there was nowhere to spend time to rest. As I didn't feel safe sleeping at night, I was exhausted during the day but as there was nowhere to sleep, I was becoming increasingly sleep deprived and exhausted.

Being homeless and having a period, especially on weekends, was awful. I couldn't stand the smell of myself and always tried to be the first in the queue at the community centre for a shower on Monday morning.

It was a horrendous existence and I missed my cat and sole companion desperately.

I decided I would take my own life, as that seemed preferable to becoming a bag-woman indefinitely.

After three days of trying to gas myself in the car, I was still alive and extremely disappointed.

I took myself to hospital as I realised I needed help and was admitted to the psychiatric ward where I spent two months.

I was then sent across the border to Queensland where they had crisis accommodation for women, even though I had intended to live in rural NSW.

After spending one month at a refuge, I then went to another that had a pet foster care program. After six months apart,

I was finally able to reunite with my cat who had been moved five times. I am still in the pet-friendly refuge and see no way of being able to exit any time soon. The Newstart benefit, currently at $670 per fortnight, makes my ability to afford housing unrealistically low. It is difficult to remain hopeful each day. The challenge is that my exit date is approaching, as I am only permitted to stay here for three months.

My mental health is very fragile as it is a stressful and chaotic environment here. All I can do is be grateful that I am with my cat and take one day at a time.

My observations: I found the public's reaction to homelessness was cold. No one approached me to offer any help, to talk to me or even bring me a hot cuppa, as it was winter. I was stared at, walked past, asked for cigarettes, asked for money, and photographed for someone's social media page. **We are just all human beings** at the end of the day and some compassion goes a long way. Services weren't much better with workers often being cold, aloof and unhelpful. I have never felt so alone and frightened before. It has changed me as a person and I hope that those who read this will change for the better, especially those who may be in a position to do something.

6. ANON

I found myself homeless and living between Salvation Army hostels and other emergency places at fourteen. Not because I didn't have anyone who loved me or a family, but because I had begun using drugs to ease the emotional discomfort I had felt since I was a very young kid. At that time, I was out of control.

From a young age I think I was sensitive, and I didn't have a way of 'dealing' with my emotions other than with what became addiction. When I experimented with drugs, I enjoyed the break from my own busy head.

The drugs made me a very different person. I became difficult to reason with and constantly felt like everyone was 'against' me. In my mind, I believed no one loved me and that I was an awful person. I continued using drugs for another ten years. I was in and out of rehab and hospital because my health would be so bad from living rough.

At twenty-four I was so desperately wanting change. I was overdosing regularly and found myself in trouble with the law.

I still had a glimmer of hope within me that life could be different. I would watch 'normal' people walk down the street going to work and with their families. I wanted that. I felt a desire in my heart for something greater, something I had never felt before.

It felt miraculous at the time when my life started to change. I began to cut down the drugs and got a 'normal' job. These were all things that felt so distant from me, yet somehow people and opportunities began to be placed in my path. In hindsight, I can see that once I felt a true desire in my heart to be a better person and to live differently, that was all I needed to start seeing other avenues in life.

Without knowing it at the time, I was so desperate that I began to reach out to something or someone for help. Now, I would call that praying to the universe or God, but at the time I had no concept of that. I was just so desperate, and asking for a better life.

Twelve years later, from back then to my life now, there have been so many amazing changes; professional and financial success, a family, children and a life void of addiction and fear. My life now feels rich with faith and endless opportunity. Today I am blessed to be able to give back where I can and am lucky enough to volunteer with Theresa at Agape, supporting others in the same situation as I once had been.

7. JUDGEMENT

I often hear about people ripping off the system, even from those in community services within other organisations.

Yes, there are people who do the wrong thing and that is sad, but need is not just about material items, sometimes what is needed, is connection.

We have to learn to recognise that a person asking for help does need 'something,' even if it may not necessarily be the material 'need' they are asking for.

Social-isolation takes the lives of thousands of people every year through suicide, so Agape embraces people in all categories of need. They are not turned away from joining our meal service just because they *can* afford to buy food. Agape is run for the homeless and needy. If a person is prepared to say they are in need, then I believe them, even if it is not a visible or tangible item. Often some of these people who may be a little 'better off' but still join our outreach, become Agape volunteers, as they realise they can add purpose and connection to their day.

In my years of outreach work, I have met many families in homes and with jobs, that still find themselves in situations where they can't afford to buy food. They are unlikely to receive help without a pension card, but does a lack of a pension card mean they are any less in need of help, even if it is just for a short time? Not in my eyes.

We have had wealthy women driving expensive cars come to us for food assistance. Often, when we say we can help, they break down crying. Many are going through divorce and their bank accounts may be frozen and government assistance isn't accessible to them yet. They can be turned away from everywhere they have gone for help just because they don't have a pension card. Their need is often for a short time, and they are usually back on their feet again pretty quickly, but for that moment they are still 'in need.'

During the COVID-19 pandemic, Agape has had high numbers of New Zealanders seeking support. Unless you have been in Australia for ten years or more, you are not entitled to government support in Australia. This means no social security payments, social housing, or pension card, which means no support from most services or discounted medical. We have had families where parents have lost their jobs during the pandemic and found themselves with no income and no support. Many of these people have been living in Australia for seven years or more but have not reached the required ten years. It is a sad fact that we have at least one family living homeless in a local park and many homeless singles, being fed by Agape.

I personally was a single mum for fifteen-and-a-half years. At one point Centrelink cut off my payments because I was working for my charity, Agape. Their theory was, and they were correct, that I spent so many hours working with Agape, it took away my ability to find full-time work. They told me to cancel the charity, quit my part-time employment, and find 'real' work.

STORIES FROM THE STREETS

I had been working part-time, and running the charity while receiving a part-payment from Centrelink. Even though I was a single mum, they stopped my payments as I would not find full-time work which would mean sacrificing time with my son, and my work with those in need.

This placed my son and I under undue financial stress, again. As I was earning less than unemployment benefit, I could apply for a healthcare card as a low-income earner. I did this once but it took months to approve, then I received one higher pay cheque and they cancelled it. I gave up on the government support and decided I would prefer to go it alone, even if it meant times of financial hardship.

The most ironic part of this is that other people can volunteer with my charity, get an exemption from looking for work, and even gain petrol allowances because of their volunteer status, while for me, as the founder and director of the charity, I can't receive any help unless I cancel everything and get a 'real' job. My 'non-real' job currently supports over 15,000 people per year and has over 150 volunteers; many of whom are registered volunteers under Centrelink.

> When no way is visible, make a way.
> -Theresa Mitchell

Anyone can be in need so please, let's not judge by appearances and give people the time to share their stories.

8. FALLING THROUGH THE CRACKS

One Wednesday night I arrived at our meal service area to find Ian having a psychotic event. While it was obvious he had been drinking, he was also hallucinating and in and out of reality. He was dancing and singing Indigenous songs while on crutches, as he had hurt his foot during the week.

Ian was completely unaware of his volume and drawing attention to himself, swinging the crutches around in the air. He was going through multiple mood changes.

Because he was drawing attention to himself in a public place, people were coming to see if they could help, but this was causing him to escalate more, as he was not used to human attention from multiple people.

Ian would never intentionally harm anyone, but the situation was pointing towards him accidentally hurting himself or someone else.

My thoughts were that it would all work out okay, as the mental health team would be there that evening. They would be able to do a case assessment and get him the help he desperately needed.

As soon as they arrived, I asked them to do a case assessment on him. As Ian's movements and volume were unpredictable, the mental health team said they needed an ambulance present before they could do anything.

So, I called an ambulance. One-and-a-half hours later, the ambulance arrived and the mental health team had gone.

I asked the paramedics if they could do a case assessment. Because Ian had been drinking and was irrational, the paramedics said they would need a police presence to be able to do anything. They called the police, who were busy at the time, and the paramedics left saying they would come back when the police were free.

Three hours passed by this time and I was still sitting beside Ian, helping to keep him isolated from the public, along with two of our other clients. They were waiting with me so that they could look after Ian's belongings if he was taken to hospital.

The homeless lose their belongings all the time in hospital or if they are taken away by police, and if their gear is left behind by itself it's likely to be either stolen or dumped in council cleanups. The guys were kindly waiting with me to protect his things from going missing.

After a while, two police cars turned up and the paramedics came back. I was pulled aside by one of the police officers and I told him that we just needed a case assessment for Ian as he was having a psychotic event. This was while another police officer tested Ian for alcohol.

The officer told me he understood what I wanted, but the paramedics would not do a case assessment because Ian was too drunk. The best they could do was take him to the station and lock him up for four hours before letting him go. I protested and explained that in four hours he would still likely be having his psychotic event and could be an unintentional harm to himself and others. He needed a diagnosis and help!

All they could do was take him to the police station.

So Ian was handcuffed, placed in the back of the police car and taken away. Four hours later he was released back onto the streets without any further help or case assessment. Of course, he did get given a $175 drunk and disorderly fine.

Three months on and Ian is now in jail, serving time because he is unable to pay his fines; fines he received from that event, and others like it.

Dual diagnoses, whether it be mental health and alcohol, alcohol and drugs, or all three together, causes a crack in the system. People are passed around in circles, with no one fixing or supporting the situation. People end up falling through the cracks every day, and dropping deeper into despair and hopelessness.

What can be done to change the system and start to help people when they actually need help? The law allows us as a community, to move people around with nothing really being done. How can we change this? This is an expense on the economy and produces greater levels of mental illness and homelessness.

If the government were to actually research the economic cost of multiple service providers, and unnecessary time in jail, I expect they would find it much cheaper to just give those in desperate need, a house and a way to support them. At present, the public service system is a black hole for finance that spends too much time just passing people back and forth.

I am thankful that Ian sent me a message from prison letting me know he is okay. I am praying that while he is there, he will get the case assessment that he needs.

9. GEORGE

George had a multimillion-dollar brokerage business, a home and a family. Things at work started to slide and George reacted to his stress levels with anger; his moods were reflected on his staff and his family.

Over time, the staff walked away, moving on to other jobs, and his wife filed for divorce. In a short period of a few months, George was bankrupt. He lost the business, his house, and his relationships with his wife, children and co-workers. He ended up living in his car on the streets.

He came to us broken and looking for a meal; hungry not just for food, but for something positive to find hope in. He did find HOPE at the street outreach. We were there with a hug, words of encouragement and a reminder that he was not alone. We were able to guide him through steps to help him move forward and to reassure him that there are things to live for.

A few months on and George has a new job, accommodation and a new love interest in his life.

I wholly believe that if there was not an organisation to meet people like George during their time of greatest need, to give them support and guidance, then stories like George's would have a very different outcome.

10. TRIGGER WARNING

Yesterday was an emotional one.

We've had an elderly gentleman visit Agape for a shower, every three to four weeks. He is very small and fragile. He can barely walk and is eating very little. We find his speech is inconsistent. We have been unable to identify where he lives, but possibly in his car, where he has no power or water access.

Our Agape case managers have put him forward for housing but nothing has come of it.

I received a call out yesterday around 1pm. This gentleman was in his car on the other side of the road to our complex, outside the courthouse. He was in the driver's seat, bent up, with his head twisted down near his right rib cage. He could still talk, inconsistently, but he could only twitch his arm and leg. A police officer had found him.

We constructed a shade with a towel to stop the sun shining on him and I sat on the roadside supporting his head and holding his hand, talking with him while we waited for an ambulance.

One of the neighbours came out and said that they had seen him in his car at 2:30am that morning. It appears he had arrived in the middle of the night to wait for a shower with Agape, and had taken a turn for the worse, while in his car. He was unable to call for help or move so he sat there, shut up in the hot car all day, until the police officer found him.

Huge praise is due to the police officer who found him and to those who stood around the car keeping the traffic away from the shoulder of the road where we were waiting for the ambulance.

The ambulance officers were great. They recognised how serious his situation was and were very empathetic to his cause. I went to the hospital and stayed with him. His blood pressure was extremely low and his organs were failing. The ER nurse was lovely and checked on me regularly, as she could see the emotional impact it was having on me.

I believe no-one should have to die alone, but no matter how many times I sit with a person holding their hand while they are dying, it always rips my heart out.

After two hours they stabilised him. His life was still hanging in the balance but he survived this time. They still have to find the cause of his illness, as without medical intervention there is no way he would have survived.

The hospital social worker told me they had raised their concerns to emergency housing, after his last visit. Six months prior he had almost died from lack of self-care, suggesting that he was unable to assist himself and needed emergency housing and support. That request had fallen on deaf ears.

Both the hospital and Agape have applied for help again but there has been no response.

He stayed in the hospital for two months where he continued to improve. They did cognitive assessments on him that showed he didn't have the mental capacity to support himself. Sadly he was released alone into homelessness with no housing and no support.

THERESA MITCHELL

Agape is still fighting, and the hospital is supporting our application to find him accommodation, but after five months, there are still no open doors. We have attempted to get him onto the NDIS, but they refuse to accept him as he is homeless. I cannot express how heart-wrenching it is to continually see such elderly, fragile people living without the basics in their last days.

A huge thank you to all the police, ambulance workers and staff at the hospital, you were fabulous and so caring. It is appreciated.

- Theresa

11. ANON

One of our patrons was sharing with me last night that the 'snakes are out.'

He and a mate were sleeping under the old church a couple of nights ago, when his mate woke up with a snake slithering across his head. Then yesterday, they were sitting beside the river behind Tweed Heads Hospital, when a red-bellied black snake chased them. They end up climbing a tree to get away.

Please pray for the safety of those less fortunate.

Photo credit to Theresa Mitchell

12. JOHN

John spent over twenty years of his life in jail and then another twenty living homeless on the streets. He has only ever known anger, crime and having to do as the authorities have told him.

He participated in a cooking program we ran for people on the streets. He loved cooking and serving the food back to others who were in the same situation as him.

After the completion of the cooking program he became a full-time 'peacekeeper' with our street program. A peacekeeper is different to a bouncer, in that they help people to stay calm. We had him make a cap with 'peacekeeper' printed on it, and this became his pride and joy. He spends his nights with us watching out for any trouble, and at the first sign of any, moves in to dissolve the issue straight away.

He now has a housing department unit and goes out of his way to help other guys and girls on the streets. He is very passionate and protective over homeless women. We could not find a more trustworthy man to work with us as our peacekeeper.

Left: Theresa Mitchell, founder of Agape Outreach Inc.
Right: Rory McDonald - Owner of Mr Rentals Tweed Heads and Lismore

13. MR RENTALS

> Mr Rentals, Tweed Heads has partnered with Agape Outreach Inc. They donate their fridges and household items to help support families setting up new homes, as they replace them in their rental business.

I was talking with one of our patrons at the outreach. He was blessed with a fridge from Mr Rental Tweed Heads, as he is setting up in a home after street life.

I knew he had been having multiple operations on his stomach and organs over the last few months, and he was telling me why. Apparently, he has gone weeks at a time without food while being homeless and it has caused serious complications internally for him.

He lost the desire to eat and said he would prefer not to. He loves the fellowship with Agape Outreach Inc. so much though he is now forcing himself to eat something and now he has a fridge, he intends to work on his eating.

Tonight he took home one lonely muffin to put in his fridge. There was plenty of food available and many things he could have taken home but he said no. He wouldn't be able to eat them, but one muffin he will. Tonight it sits in his fridge alone and waiting, and to him it is a positive symbol of his appetite returning.

14. TIM

When Tim started to come along to the evening meals, he was very quiet and reserved. After he had attended a few times I asked him if he would like to take some left over bread to feed to the birds, as I was aware he was an animal lover.

He accepted and that week while he had been feeding the birds the old bread, a German backpacker had approached him asking for food, saying that he was starving and had not eaten for days.

Tim felt overwhelming compassion for the young man whose mates had gone on ahead of him. His car had broken down and he had no money until his mates planned to return in a fortnight.

Tim took him under his wing, bringing him to Agape for free meals and even sleeping near him to make sure he was safe until the return of his friends.

During this time Tim blossomed and really started to open up. He said to me one night, 'Theresa, I remember now. Six months ago I was standing in my kitchen with the shopping bags in my hands, when I received a phone call to say that my wife and son were dead, killed in a car accident by a drunk driver. I put the shopping bags down on the floor and walked out the back door.' He had no memories of the previous six months until the simple act of giving woke him up.

Tim found that he was on the missing persons list and he has now contacted his extended family. He has started the process of healing, all because he experienced the receiving and giving of love.

15. TARA

Tara was only fifteen when she decided that her new stepfather's rules at home were too much to bear and the freedom of her natural father's life style of living on the streets was appealing for her.

Her natural father explained that the stress of his business and pressure from meeting expectations of the world had been too great. He now had the freedom to live how he desired and in the open was all he could dream of.

Tara was more than willing to fall into this new lifestyle and she partied hard every night. Drinking and drugs became a regular habit and so did waking up in different men's beds. It didn't take long before the lack of home comfort and safety kicked in. Tara would spend her time at the outreach crying on our shoulder wanting to go home but being too ashamed.

Unfortunately she now found herself in a place where addiction drove her decisions. She was using sex in exchange for drugs and was even fearful for her life. Her choices were no longer her own with the men she was with.

Being only fifteen, she was too young for rehab, as you need to be over eighteen. Foster care wouldn't take her because she didn't meet the requirements of 'at risk,' as she wasn't being beaten and she was 'too old.' In their opinion, she was considered to be turning sixteen soon, even though she had only just turned fifteen, and at sixteen she would go back to the streets and doing her own thing, so they wouldn't accept her. I was an intensive needs foster carer with no children in my care at that time, but they still wouldn't accept her. So we worked with her parents and had her admitted to the mental illness section of the hospital, while she detoxed from drugs. Tara was diagnosed with 'drug-induced Bipolar' and after a couple of months she was able to return home.

She educated herself at home and was able to sit her grade ten school certificate. I had the pleasure of supervising her exam. She put in every effort she could muster and passed the exam. Some of the other teens in the exam just wrote their name on the top of the paper and put their heads on the desk and fell asleep. Not Tara, she gave it her all and I was so proud.

Today at twenty-six years old, Tara has a job, a steady boyfriend and they just purchased a house. She is very happy in her new lifestyle and most importantly she is safe.

Her natural father found some shared accommodation and started a new business after Tara came off the streets; he turned away from street life as the cost on his daughter was too much to bear. He visited me when he recieved his first pay and donated it to us as a thank you for helping Tara get her life back.

16. ANON

Growing up in the '80s I recall constantly being told by people, 'Don't do drugs, drugs are bad.' But at the tender age of twelve, I ran away from home and had my very first encounter with drugs, which taught me that those people had all been wrong. In fact, I found that drugs made me feel very good. By the age of thirteen I was drinking heavily and smoking marijuana regularly. I was in trouble at school and with the police.

Some nights I slept on the streets, in alleyways, school cubby houses, on public transport, in underage night clubs, anywhere I felt safe to close my eyes. On my fourteenth birthday I woke up on the lounge room floor of a friend, and her mum let me stay there as long as I supplied her marijuana.

I was homeless, not because I didn't have a home, but because life on the streets was more appealing than my house and family.

During the following year I began to break into houses and crudely manufacture drugs to sell at a local high school. I was snorting speed and smoking marijuana daily. I unwillingly lost my virginity. I started private kickboxing lessons and to gain practice and vent my anger I would start fights, but on the streets there were no rules, and at times I had to literally fight for my life, or run and hide.

THERESA MITCHELL

At fifteen, I was groomed by a much older man. Ralph was involved with bikies, organised crime and had a bad reputation. He offered accommodation to me and devastatingly introduced me to heroin. After a bad experience in a car I had stolen for an organised group I was working with, I began to question my lifestyle. I was desperately unhappy and had begun to feel paranoid, as if I was being watched and listened to. I hated the person I had become and felt I had no way out of my situation. Rejected by my family and alone, apart from the criminals and drug addicts I was surrounded by, I attempted to overdose. I thought I would be better off dead than to continue going down the path I was on. My overdose attempt failed.

My anguish did not subside, nor did my drug addiction. I was so desperate and as a cry for help I called my mother. She reiterated her disgust and loathing of me and I felt I could sink no lower. I vividly remember sitting at Ralph's kitchen table and a wretched and uncontrolled howl came out of me; a sorrow and brokenness. I had hit rock bottom.

Not long after that, Ralph spoke to me about my call to my mother, and my ensuing emotional grief, and I realised my paranoia was, in fact, real. Ralph had been watching my every move.

Distraught, I called my former social worker. Peg had previously been assigned to me from some trouble with the police I had a few years earlier. I called Peg from Ralph's house, but another lady answered the phone and advised me that Peg had left the organisation. My heart sank. She was also a social worker but she worked in a different department, on a different floor and had no idea why she answered the phone on someone else's desk on that particular day. I told her very bluntly why I was calling and she responded immediately by gaining emergency authorisation to work with me.

She offered to help me relocate to a safe house as well as get me into rehab. The next few hours were terrifying. She came and met me at Ralph's house, I packed a few things and as we were backing out of the driveway in her car, to my horror, she stopped. She wanted me to be sure I was leaving because I wanted to, and to make the point that this was my decision.

I was taken to a halfway house an hour and a half drive out of the city, but within a month Ralph had found me. It was arranged for me to hide at the house of friend of one of her family members. She helped me to apply for rehab but there was a four to six month wait period. I was still using a lot of drugs, but I had managed to detox myself from heroin and was only using it occasionally.

I got a part-time job at a lunch bar and started seeing a new guy. He was quiet and gentle and liked to surf. He was travelling around Australia.

As the months passed, I began for the first time in many years, to feel hopeful about the future but a few medical issues arose and I decided to go a doctor. I had shared so many needles over the last few years and had a lot of unprotected, and at times, non-consensual sex, so I assumed that I had contracted some kind of disease. In fact, I was miraculously disease free, but I was pregnant.

I told him, and he made it very clear he was not ready to be a father. At this point our relationship ended. Unfortunately by this stage, Ralph had found me again and now I had to leave that city and go into hiding until a place became available in rehab.

THERESA MITCHELL

It was years later that my friend, the social worker, told me her boss had threatened to let her go, because in her twenty-year career as a government social worker, she had never crossed the line professionally, but with me she had become attached. At one point, she had even planned to hide me at her own house.

I was in rehab for three months and against all the doctors' and nurses' advice, I did not have an abortion. That little baby was the lifeline that gave me the incentive to never use drugs again.

I have been clean twenty years now - totally drug free. Where I was once a homeless, drug-addicted criminal, I am now recovered; a mother, a wife and a friend who contributes to society and my community around me.

17. BEYOND YOURSELF

Every day we have the opportunity to stand up for something or someone; we are given a reason to think beyond ourselves. I believe the majority of us manifest an idea, a way to make a difference, yet sadly very few of us ever see it through to fruition.

We may even recognise the calling in our heart that we can make a change, yet in most cases, a transition takes place, where we begin thinking about ourselves again, rather than the person in need. Fear kicks in and we become desperate to protect ourselves. In some cases, we can even becoming defensive about helping this person, or believe it would diminish us, or our reputation, somehow.

Our imagination can be our worst enemy if we let it. It robs us of our true calling in life. With any positive change, you don't need to know how, just start and see where it takes you.

18. MAX

This story is about the gentlest, most placid person that you will ever be blessed to meet. He is a true-blue Aussie swaggie. He has no addictions or ailments but he loves street life.

On asking him what it is about homelessness that he loves so much, Max tells me, 'It's the freedom; not being tied to anything or anyone. I was married once and had a child, but they moved away to Canada and truthfully, while I like people, I prefer to not have to deal with the issues that come with them.'

Max has been on the streets for over twenty years. He lives on the Gold Coast in the summer and goes to Cairns for the warmth in winter each year.

He has a little bedsit on call for the days that he feels he needs to be inside, but they are few and far between.

The openness and the freedom of being where he wants, when he wants and to literally disappear when he wants, calls to Max daily and he wouldn't have it any other way.

Ronnie: photo credit to Theresa Mitchell

19. RONNIE

Ronnie had no family and grew up in orphanages. His experience wasn't a good one, leaving him believing that no-one cared for him and that he couldn't trust anyone because they would hurt or abuse him.

This pain in one so young, led to a life of crime spanning decades, with alternate bouts of being homeless versus time in prison.

Ronnie got sick and tired of being sent to jail, so he went on the run. For fifteen-and-a-half years, he ran from the law. During this period he tells the story of when he became a 'proper' alcoholic and he knew that his anger was eating him up.

One day he decided enough was enough. He stopped fighting the internal emotions and the external rules. He handed himself in and cleared his debt with the law. He became a lay preacher in jail, sharing forgiveness, and he never returned to drinking.

He has spent no less than twenty years on the streets, and maybe a lot more as he has lost count.

Ronnie's whole life, sadly, is only filled with memories of street life and jail time, void of a family and loved ones. Despite this start in life, he turned away from self-pity and started to support others.

He now lives in a housing department house and works as volunteer peacekeeper, breaking up fights at the homeless meals services. He considers himself to be a protector of the people who cannot protect themselves. He has adopted the homeless and the meal providers as his family.

Ronnie's message to others:

'You have to be positive and change for yourself regardless of circumstances. I believe in God and I believe that God is in everything I do. I also believe in myself.

'It's hard sometimes, but you have to find people you can trust. I have found them, so you can too.'

While Ronnie is a funny character, who can fit more 'f-bombs' into a sentence than cheese on a pizza, he also has a heart that longs to love people. He has turned his pain into a gift that shines and makes people smile.

Agape Outreach Inc. conducted a wedding for a homeless couple a few years back and Ronnie was asked to be the best man. He could not have been prouder. He bought a six-dollar suit from the op shop and had dentures made to wear with the suit. (See photo). Those dentures live permanently in the suit pocket and only come out on rare and special occasions.

Photo credit to Theresa Mitchell

20. GAYLE

Gayle came to the streets around three years ago. Her marriage had broken down and she found herself homeless. She was very positive and fixed on getting off the streets within the next three months.

Then the negativity and hopelessness of her situation took its toll. Mental illness took a hold of her, and depression moved into schizophrenia.

Sadly, Gayle no longer eats because she believes, without a doubt, that no-one can ever care for her and that people will only hurt her.

She has been diagnosed with advanced cancer and it is just a matter of time now before she is taken to hospital for her last trip.

Homelessness has claimed another angel. :(

21. CAROL

Carol grew up in Coolangatta and worked in her parents' Chinese resturant.

All through primary school, she was teased and bullied, even in boarding school where she only stayed for two terms. The lasting effects of her emotional and unsettled childhood stuck with her into adulthood.

Carol first became homeless with her little miniature fox terrier back in Christmas 1994. This lasted for eight years until she managed to save enough money to buy a caravan with her disability pension and set up a little home.

In 2015, Carol's new boyfriend kicked her out of the caravan; he kept it and all of her belongings. She was homeless again and left with nothing.

She has been on the housing deptment list since 1994 and after this experience, returned looking for help again.

Carol was told that they couldn't help her or speed up the process, so she should 'go find a private rental.' Having no rental history references and coming from a background of homelesness, this was next to impossible. She moved from one temporary accomodation to the next over the coming years.

Carol attributes her strong resilience to having helped her

to survive and not lose hope while everything around her was uncertain.

After twenty-four years on the housing department list, she has finally been accepted into housing. Carol had been living in a cheap motel with holes through the floor boards, where they turned the water off at 6pm every night. It was dirty and the some of the other residents were scary.

She is so happy to again have a home of her own and she believes that her past trials have made her stronger.

Carol: photo credit to Theresa Mitchell

Photo credit to Theresa Mitchell

22. JACOB

Jacob was the funniest drunk on the block.

After being a foster child and moving multiple times in his life, he had a gaping hole in his heart for love.

He drank to console this, but as he told me regularly, it's okay because he is such a nice drunk.

Jacob was used to the police constantly coming by and watching him just to give him a 'move on' notice, so he created the 'crab dance.' He would scuttle along the floor with his pinchers up, singing and dancing to perform for them. This mostly resulted in them ignoring him.

When I first met Jacob, he was so drunk that he would fall unconscious into his soup and we would clean him up and stop him from drowning in it.

I've had many visits to the hospital to help him; once after he had put his arm through a glass window and cut the tendons in his arm, another when he fell down a flight of stairs and broke his leg.

Over time, he drank less, but he just couldn't shake it. He would cook in our cooking class and joined our outings. We helped him to get his story featured in *New Idea* magazine and he juggled for their photos. He was respectful when actively participating in Agape's activities, and never drank enough alcohol to fall unconscious again when he was with us.

Jacob was 'that' guy who would ring me from the disabled toilet floor at midnight just to say, 'Hi, what ya doing? I'm bored.'

In time, he found himself a girlfriend; a homeless woman who was a heavy drug user. Jacob had never used drugs because his thing was alcohol.

Their relationship was toxic; fighting all the time. She hated to see him vomit, which would happen each morning when he woke because his body had started to detox from the alcohol while he was sleeping. She would tell him to drink more so he wouldn't vomit.

One night, she overdosed and went into a coma. I attended her bedside while they turned off the machine and I met her eleven siblings who screamed 'WHY?'

While I know I shouldn't think that way, I did wonder where they had been for the last year while she was using a public disabled toilet as her home.

Jacob was distraught and felt completely lost after she was gone. His only focus was on how much love he had lost.

It was about two weeks later when I received the call to say that Jacob had been completely depressed the night before, and someone had offered him drugs. He went against his own beliefs and took the drugs that ended his life.

His body was found in the public disabled toilet that morning and I was needed to identify him.

When a homeless person dies and there is no one to collect them, someone needs to identify the body. The body is then sent for a pauper's funeral where they are cremated and the ashes are disposed of.

STORIES FROM THE STREETS

I identified his body and found his natural father. His father had been out of the country and had not had contact with him in years.

He was very distraught when he received the news of his son, so we supported him and helped to make funeral arrangements. His father wished for him to have a funeral for the street people, as they were his friends.

Agape conducted the funeral and Jacob had ninety people come to say goodbye. They had all loved him dearly. He will be remembered for the crab dance and his cheeky smile.

Jacob is greatly missed and there is no one else who has filled his shoes of the funniest drunk in town.

23. ANON

One of our male clients was in a conversation with a volunteer when I noticed his eyes go watery while he was talking to her. He then removed the leash from his dog's collar, wrapped it around his own neck and started to pull tight.

I jumped into the conversation quickly and proceeded to talk him down.

Shortly after, another volunteer, who must have also noticed his actions, came over with a bag of muffins for him. He expressed thanks and hugged her, but said he only liked mud cake.

She told him she could help him with that and walked off with the bag. I continued to talk to him and he removed the leash from his neck.

Meanwhile she returned with mud cakes for him. He teared up again looking at her and asked her if he could call her aunty, as he loved her and wanted her as his family.

Now she was all teared up.

This is what it's about! Making a difference in a person's life, no matter how small. We never know when a caring action from a volunteer might save a life or give a chance for someone to remember that there are people who care. It is beautiful for the volunteers to see that their love in action can have a life-changing effect.

With the first wall broken down for this client, he took the step of allowing himself to trust again. Over the years, we have built a great friendship, and ten years on he has just received housing.

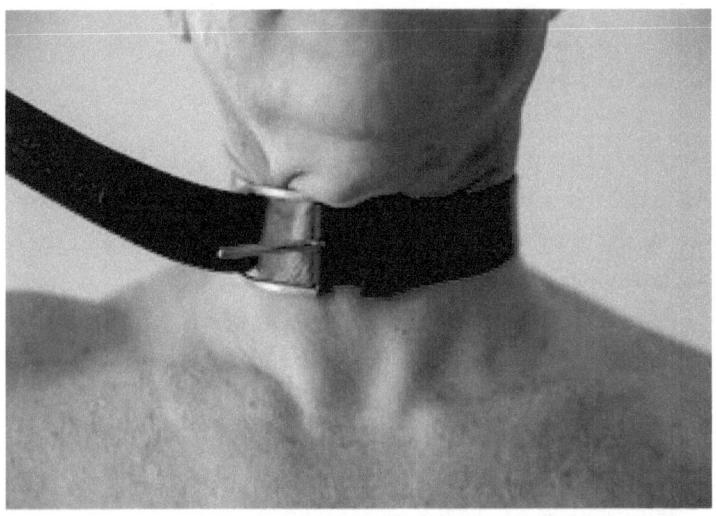

Photo credit to Jessica Brown Photography

24. EVE

Eve has been a part of our meal service for the last twelve years, the whole time we have been operating. We've had many conversations but they are all jumbled stories of her past and some obviously delusional stories too.

We know that she sleeps rough around the airport district and that she goes through the rubbish bins looking for food and cigarettes when she can't access food through a service.

One of her friends identified to us that she receives no benefits from the government and therefore cannot be on a housing list.

When we speak with her, she tells of writing choreography for ballet at the Opera House and living in a penthouse with friends overlooking Coolangatta.

Then the stories jump to the hospital owing her a unit and the keys are coming, but there's a hold up until next week.

We've had Centrelink staff talk with her on many occasions but because she tells them she is working and living in a penthouse, they will not help.

Four years ago, Agape was tagged in a post on social media of a daughter looking for her mum and she had a photo of Eve.

I contacted her and we were able to fill in some of the blanks.

Her daughter, now nineteen and a young mother, wanted

to find her mum again. As far back as she could remember, Eve was telling stories of alien abductions and walking out of the house for days at a time, leaving her father to raise her, and her siblings, alone.

They had Eve assessed and a diagnosis was made sixteen years ago, but Eve's daughter couldn't remember the outcome or who would have made the assessment.

The only way to get an assessment which may lead to her accessing payments, is to have her incarcerated in a mental hospital. This is a serious process with many rights being removed for the person. So far, no-one in her circles wants to lose her trust by putting her through this.

It was a slow process with the two of them meeting, as Eve remembered her daughter as a three-year-old girl and not a nineteen-year-old woman with a child. But over time, she came to realise that this was her daughter and she accepted them.

Eve still doesn't have any identifying paperwork, a usable diagnosis, social security payments or housing, but she does have the holiday seasons visiting with her daughter and granddaughter, and at least she knows where her mum is. She also knows that people are looking out for her in the best way they can.

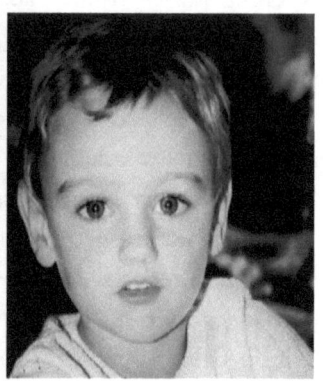

25. RUCKUS

I learnt from a young age that the only consistency in life is change. I was the youngest of four children; second child in my mother's second marriage.

My father was an interstate truck driver, with long stints away from home. We regularly moved around to accommodate the company he worked for.

My older brother, Dave, and sister, Mandy, from my mother's first marriage, lived with us until I was about four or five years old.

My sister had attempted suicide a few times and on a couple of occasions my brother, Chris, and I had come home from school to find our mother unconscious on her bed, taking what I presume would have been prescription meds.

There was a falling-out between my father and my mother's firstborn children, and I later learned he was sexually and mentally abusing them both. Dave and Mandy moved away and we had little contact with them until I was around seven years old.

My father had a significant truck accident just before I was born and received a payout when I was around seven.

Mum and dad then bought a house and car and for a moment, a fleeting moment, I thought (as much as a child does), that there finally might be some normality to life; no more moving, no more new schools, just stability.

We settled in to a small town in coastal, country Victoria. One afternoon after school, walking home from the bus stop, there were a few cars parked in our driveway.

Chris and I walked in and mum was at the dinner table, red-eyed and shaking. I'll never forget the words she breathed. 'Dave's dead.' My heart broke; firstly for my mum, and secondly for myself. He seemed an adult to me, however looking back, he was just a boy. Eighteen years young, and he died from a heroin overdose.

Later, I learned that mum, dad and Dave had made plans for us to move to Melbourne and for him to come home and live with us.

My dad started driving and was away quite a lot. It was 1995 when he started driving a truck for a friend of his. My brother, Chris, and I frequently joined him on his trips, sometimes going a few days without food, and watching dad take any number of amphetamines to stay awake and being rather short-tempered with two kids in the truck.

Being in the truck with dad, we learnt he had a young girlfriend in Queensland who he'd been seeing and staying with while he was away.

I don't believe in 'good' or 'evil,' however, if I was to label a human as evil, it'd be my dad.

My brother and I were told to keep it a secret from our mother, naturally. Dad would explain to my brother at great lengths what it was to 'be in love.' He decided the time had come to leave our mother and start a new life with his girlfriend

STORIES FROM THE STREETS

in Queensland. What he hadn't anticipated though, was mum telling him to take us with him.

He told all his fellow driving buddies that his best friend, Simon, had been sleeping with my mum, and that's why they split.

The day we left, he gave mum a small bottle of pills and said it'd be best for everyone if she took a few and had a long sleep. What a guy.

Once in Queensland, my brother and I hung out at his new girlfriend's parents' warehouse. It was a long time before we were enrolled into school. It was horrible. She forced us to call her 'mum.' We begged to go home to Melbourne, and dad wasn't happy about that. We finally convinced mum to let us come home and caught a Greyhound bus from Queensland to Melbourne; just us kids, alone.

We got home to Melbourne and learnt that Mum and Simon had formed a relationship and are still together to this day. They weren't in a position to care for us, so we got shipped off to Adelaide with one of mum's friends; a transvestite prostitute called Ashley.

We lived in a small unit in Adelaide, with another transvestite prostitute who dealt drugs from the lounge room and ate out of a homeless shelter.

Ashley was sexually inappropriate with me and I was too young to know I could stop it, but old enough to know it was wrong.

I'm not sure how long we were there, but Ashley got a call from mum and next thing we knew, we were going home. Mum and Simon had moved, again. When we got to the new place, mum sat us down to tell us our dad had died. Great!

After the funeral and several more moves and schools, mum and Simon bought a house and we finally had some form of stability. We settled into the neighbourhood and our schools, made friends and started to have a somewhat normal life.

My older sister, Mandy, was now married with two kids and started talking with my mother again to rebuild some form of relationship.

Shortly after her marriage, she skipped town with her drug dealer, moved to Adelaide and gassed herself in a car, leaving her new husband and two daughters behind.

I was heartbroken.

We went on the move again and again. Drifting from country Victoria to northern NSW. Starting new schools, especially high school, is a tough gig.

It was in northern NSW that I decided I was done with the nomad life. I was all of fifteen. I'd met some friends and found a groove in music that I wasn't prepared to leave behind. Surprisingly, my parents decided to move again. Not for me this time.

I moved in with my best friend's family for a while until I found a one-bedroom flat. I was going to school, living on my own and drinking heavily. I was politely asked to leave school and didn't need to be asked twice.

I was fortunate enough to get an apprenticeship and start working full-time, which was handy, since I had a drinking habit to support. I was living with my girlfriend at the time and life was okay - until she moved home and my heart was broken. Young love!

I couldn't afford rent on my own, so instead of moving or getting a flatmate, I spent my money on booze, to the point where I was late for work and even lost track of days. I was evicted and found myself couch surfing. Slowly working my way through my small list of friends for somewhere to stay, until they were all used up.

Being proud, I was not going to be a burden on anyone anymore, so I found myself sleeping in a Vinnies donation bin, washing my clothes and showering at work. My boss caught on and wasn't too impressed. He gave me an ultimatum: sort my shit out or fuck off.

He was kind enough to let me sleep on his couch for a while until I found a room to rent.

But then I moved to the Gold Coast with some friends from high school and started a band. I got a job in a workshop there and skipped work pretty frequently to drink and play music. Needless to say, the job didn't last long. Here I was again, just turned twenty-one with no job, drinking addictively and couch surfing among friends.

The week of my twenty-first birthday, I was fired, and I thought I'd party til the following week before looking for another job. My housemates had other ideas. I was kicked out, drunk, upset and had nowhere to go.

I filled my car with my meagre possessions and started driving south to where my parents had ended up. I don't remember how, but I woke up seven hours from the Gold Coast with a headache and an empty tank.

I spent a few months back in Victoria before deciding my heart was on the coast. I convinced my brother to come with me and with $500 between us, we left. We arrived with no jobs or a place to live and of course, we were drunk.

Chris lasted a month. We were sleeping on the couch of my drummer and good friend Vincent's parents' house. They were beautiful to us and it was his mother that taught me to meditate and to heal my heart.

Chris moved back to Victoria and I was too proud to keep crashing at my friend's house, so I lied and said I had found a place. I slept in my car for two weeks while working as a telemarketer.

With the help of Vincent's mother, I began to meditate daily. I focused on forgiving myself and those who I held hate towards in my heart. During mediation, I shifted from victim to gratitude.

I'm now thirty-two and going through an interesting divorce. I just completed my studies in Life and Wellness Coaching and have toured the country a number of times with my band. I am blessed to have been to South East Asia and to have worked in the orphanages that rescue young kids from slavery. I have even worked with the Gold Coast City Council on a couple of youth initiatives.

I'm not immune to feelings of utter hopelessness, as I sometimes close my eyes and the past flickers by, bringing painful stabs to my heart. I see flashes of my brother, Dave's, face, I sometimes see my sister, Mandy, holding her daughter and it still hurts.

These experiences have led me to take responsibility for my own mental and emotional wellness. I can't change the things that happened to me as a child, and I don't think I would if I could.

I have a heart full of gratitude and a firm belief that you can't fully know and understand the hot, without first experiencing cold.

-Ruckus

26. ANON

At the age of forty-one, I became homeless in my hometown of Byron Bay where I worked and lived in the shire for seventeen years.

I feel it's important to disclose the sexual abuse I experienced at seven years old, by a family friend, and the verbal and physical abuse I received from all the members of my family, except my father.

I found refuge in drugs and alcohol from the age of thirteen. I used every drug around in the '70s, and left home at sixteen. I flitted my way through many jobs, and helped other lost souls not unlike myself along the way.

We all had a common thread stemming from childhood; being abused. I tried to commit suicide twice but I praise God it was a cry for help and I never needed to go to hospital. I actually overdosed on heroin twice, but my friends (I call them friends, others call them junkies), brought me back to life. I loved my buddies and lost too many of them to the demon of drugs.

We used to self-medicate to bury the pain we couldn't tolerate. When I fell pregnant at twenty-one I went straight and sobered up for the first time since I was thirteen. The world seemed so much brighter and lighter. I knew I would do everything I could to protect my baby from experiencing the same abuse I had suffered. Sadly though, the father of my baby was very controlling and belittling of me. I studied, ran my own businesses, and had a perfect baby, but my partner put me down daily.

A traumatic experience of a home invasion at our expensive Dover Heights home put me through the ordeal of having a double-barrelled shotgun pointed at my head. After this experience I sought counselling and over time found the courage to leave my partner. I packed up my baby and my belongings and headed north to the Byron Shire. I was a single parent entrenched in trauma, grief and loss, however, my child's wellbeing and safety was my only priority.

I secured a department of housing home (DOH) for myself and my child. I worked hard, studied and worked in Community Services; I worked in drug and alcohol support, was also a dance/eerobic/fitness instructor and worked as a personal trainer. Over this time I suffered more traumas that I won't go into, but grief and loss surrounded my life, my mind, my soul and my body.

I raised my daughter as a single parent, rarely asking for help outside of counselling, as I really didn't trust anyone.

My daughter left home when she turned eighteen to study in Sydney. I became a born-again Christian and found my higher power. Even though I always knew God, this was different.

I was offered a job in Thailand in a five-star hotel as a fitness director. I wanted to rent my DOH home in Byron Bay out to a single parent for the year contract, however they gave me the wrong information and said I couldn't do that.

STORIES FROM THE STREETS

Upon returning from Thailand four months later, I collected my Rottweiler from my daughter in Sydney and headed back to Byron Bay, only to find the boom in real estate had happened. I couldn't afford to buy my dream home.

I took the DOH to the tribunal and won. They said I was now on the priority list for Byron Bay for a one-bedroom flat. I have never lived in a flat in my life as I can't be close to people or loud noise. These are triggers for my PTSD.

I could not find an affordable place in Byron Bay as I had a dog, no job, and no rental references except for my time in the DOH, which apparently looks bad to rental agents.

I slept in my car with my dog, and camped in a tent in the bush. Many of the homeless were my ex-clients from an Aboriginal rehab I used to work in. They became my new friends and looked out for my safety. However, at times I was threatened and verbally abused by the some of the non-Aboriginal homeless people.

I dated an Aboriginal Arawkal man whose family and mob became my family. I was extremely close to his mother who offered me shelter in her home when I was homeless. She became my mentor, my aunty and my closest and dearest friend.

Each of the homeless had their stories of how and why they became homeless. A lot were well educated, served in the Vietnam War and were either sexually, physically or mentally abused as children by the people they trusted; their parents or in the foster homes they were sent to by the government.

Many of my friends from pre-homelessness thought I had lost the plot, as I sat in the park some days with the parkies, listening to their music and stories, sharing in a joint, bourbon or Valium.

One of my counsellors at the time when I disclosed that I had been using again said, 'Isn't that a song.' I replied, 'No, but I can write one for you.'

The parkies used to mind my dog most days while I looked for employment and accommodation. They loved my dog and treated him with kindness and love; Mardie gave them so much joy. A year later most of the parkies had a beloved dog themselves, and what a difference unconditional love from a pet made in their lives. They had smiles on their faces every day. They made sure they had money to feed them and take them to the vet. I also noticed their drugs and alcohol consumption had slowed down as their pet was their priority.

Unable to find accommodation or a job in welfare in Byron Shire, I secured job placements in the Aboriginal communities in Alice Springs, in the East Kimberley's, and the Thursday Islands. I loved working and living in the dry communities of Australia. However, being only contract work and being so far from my daughter, I returned home again to Byron Bay.

I returned to Byron, to a friend's home where I was able to secure jobs in housekeeping, in cafés, driving taxis and hired cars. After waiting on the list for fourteen years, I was offered a government housing flat, which I had to accept as rentals were just unaffordable.

In the units above me and to one side, resided ice dealers. I hardly slept during the two years I lived there. I rang the police constantly with the issues going on. I was assaulted by an ice addict, and my car was doused with brake fluid. The department of housing finally moved me up north, closer to my daughter and my new grandchildren on the Gold Coast.

Once again I found myself in a flat with ice dealers and users around me. The antisocial behaviour around the units was the same. I took out a protection order against my neighbour who threatened to cut my throat. I had called the police on him many times for physically abusing his girlfriend. I took videos but nothing was done and she was found bashed and dead in his apartment.

He became a person of interest in her manslaughter. The police interviewed me, took the videos as evidence and again I was placed on a priority transfer to a new unit in Tweed Heads. I put in for a mutual exchange and found a great case worker at Social Futures, who is also my disability employment case worker. He also became my advocate for my rights against housing and their lack of duty of care.

Recently I was blessed through a three-way mutual exchange to a two-bedroom villa in a quiet street with only one other villa in front. I will be able to sleep every night. I will study again and go for job interviews. My grandkids will be able to come and stay.

My case worker and I did the work. Housing failed to follow their own policies or procedures and many of the staff are rude, and inadequately trained. It felt like I was nothing but a bother to them. I have many complaints and will be taking my mistreatment further.

Legal aid has just sent me an email and given me all the information I need to take housing to the tribunal for their lack of duty of care and the loss of my earnings because I was unable to sleep well during the five years residing in my flat surrounded by antisocial behaviour and late night parties.

I have returned to my faith and can honestly say that without my prayers and my new church friends, I wouldn't have thought that staying in a nice home again was possible. Thank you God. Always fight for your rights and never give up on what you are truly worth.

Blessings.

Photo credit to Shaun Lister

27. HOMELESSNESS - A PRICE TO PAY

Nobody likes to see homeless people out on the streets; oh ... they are best left sight unseen.

Remember, that could be YOU!

Homelessness can happen to anyone, rich or poor.

Homelessness has always been a sight preferred to be unseen.

My story is not dissimilar to others, but it is always a challenge to keep striving for a better life out there. I don't know what keeps me going, just maybe a faith that things will get better.

I found myself in a downward spiral out of my control. First of all, I was going through the grief of my mother's death when that escalated into a family 'falling out' crisis. Little did I know, I would find myself in a homeless situation, which was quite foreign to me. Never in my wildest dreams would I have seen myself living this way.

If someone with a crystal ball told me that in ten years I would be in such a situation I would never have believed it would be me - but it was!

With nowhere to live, and after several suicide attempts, I

was a physical and mental wreck. As ridiculous as it sounds, the only friend I could count on - was my car.

It was a roof over my head and a place to sleep. The car was reliable enough to take me where I needed to go. I consider myself as being one of the lucky ones. Living in my car and 'sorta' having a roof over my head is lucky, when compared with sleeping rough on the streets.

Either way, it is a hardship relying on social services, homeless outreach centres and charities for the basics in life like food, shelter and a shower. Homelessness is losing your dignity and self-worth.

Here lies the question of homelessness; the how, what and where?

How does it exist?

What can we do about it?

Where to house or where to build?

Can we please get a symposium on housing/renting affordability to be put on the table with government, to get real answers from the states, local councils, developers and architects with some innovative ideas to solve what is a growing problem?

Homelessness is the price we pay when rent affordability is out of the question.

Rent affordability is becoming increasingly harder, as wage growth has slowed down, and in today's work environment, full-time work has become a rarefied ideal, making part-time and casual work the norm.

Let's get smart people with smart ideas making something happen, instead of empty words from out-of-touch politicians.

The great divide between rich and poor is bigger than ever, and housing is the basic human right to be achieved here; to have a roof over your head, a safe place for you and your belongings and, of course, your dignity and self-worth, to attain what is commonly called a home.

Sadly, for some, that will never happen. What kind of society have we become, when our children's children won't have the same opportunities unless they are rich?

No-one wants to know about this and it's not really on the national agenda, because they believe it will never happen to them! The reality is that it could and it does happen to many!

- Jeff Lutter

28. DAVID

David came up to me one day at a homeless convention. The council puts on yearly homeless conventions in an attempt that they can connect easily with services.

This day he came to me and said he had just been to visit the housing stall and had good news.

He calls me the Vicar.

'Vicar,' he says. 'Good news. I've been on the streets for twenty-three years and in seven years time I will be eighty years old. That's when housing will make a priority of me and I can get a house.'

David is seventy-three years old, and a grandfather who has no substance issues, he just can't afford housing.

He has to wait another seven years for help.

29. FAYE'S STORY

We first heard about Faye from some of our homeless guys sleeping rough. They said that she was sixty-eight years old and living under the mangroves in a drain pipe amongst them. They said that youths had come by the other day throwing rocks into the camp. The guys were very upset that Faye could be hurt by these youth. I encouraged them to bring Faye down to meet us.

After a few weeks, Faye started attending the free meal service. She was small in stature and looked so fragile. Faye looked as though she could be someone's grandma and our heart broke for her.

After a little while she started to trust us and we attempted to get her into housing. She was very scared to leave her camp as she felt people would steal her only belongings. She was also an insulin-dependent diabetic and epileptic so she didn't want to go far from the local hospital.

First, we managed to get her into shared accommodation on weekends during winter; low drops in temperature can claim the fragile lives of the elderly. Faye loved the older lady she was staying with but she was too concerned about her belongings and returned to the street during the week.

We then managed to get her into a motel room over some of

the coldest nights of winter. She really enjoyed the independent living and during this time started to share her story.

Faye's daughter had suffered from a rare form of cancer and had passed away at thirty-one years old. Faye didn't cope well over this period and she lashed out with anger, as she could not comprehend why her daughter would pass away before her.

After this period, Faye still grief-ridden, became very sick and was admitted to hospital where she fell into a coma for a couple of weeks. When she came out of the coma, the staff at the hospital told her that her husband had not visited once.

Faye took herself home after being discharged and told him that she wanted a divorce. Her husband then forced her outside the front door and locked it in her face.

Faye had nothing, no clothing, no medication; nothing. She called the police and they went onto the property to retrieve her medication, but that was all.

For two years, Faye managed living in a boarding house which she found scary and unsafe as they were extremely run-down living conditions. After this she decided it would be cheaper and possibly safer to sleep rough, hidden away from people.

She moved into a water drain pipe, and this is where she would live for the next nine months.

The rough-sleeping guys around her were all on ice but they saw her as their mother and tried to protect her from youth gangs and anyone else who might harm her. Faye also felt like a mother to them, and in this strange situation she felt safe.

Faye ended up finding her own permanent shared accommodation; the rental price was cheaper as it included support work to help look after a disabled lady in her eighties. The woman's daughter lived next door and needed someone to help support her mum.

Faye settled in there, and helping to look after someone seemed to be just what she needed to move past her own fears and distrust of people. Once settled and feeling safe again, Faye wanted to help educate the public that homeless people are everyday people going through hard times, to gain more support and to give a message to those on the street that it's okay to trust people again.

Faye allowed Agape to make a short film on her story to raise this awareness. Actors are used in the documentary, as the story was too painful for Faye to re-enact herself.

Faye's story can be found on you tube at:
https://www.youtube.com/watch?v=KII51ldZLlQ
Credits to Sunny Day films and Whitney Palmer Photography for making the documentary.

Photo credit to Shaun Lister

30. MELISSA GROOM

Mums in Business, Social influencer, SYDNEY CITY MISSION - Youth Refuge RADIO HOUSE

At the age of sixteen, as I was just about to start my final year in high school, I found myself homeless.

No, I wasn't a naughty kid or a troublemaker and I didn't get kicked out of home. In fact, I was picked up from school by the department of welfare.

I will never forget the day. I had started a new school and a young girl came up to me at lunchtime to say, 'The school counsellor wants to see you.' I must have looked a little alarmed. 'Don't worry. It's just a standard thing we do for new students to give them a welcome.'

As I walked into the school office and down the hallway I was not aware my life was about to change significantly. It was one of the most defining moments of my life.

The young student escorted me to the office, knocked on the door of the school counsellor and then said, 'There you go,' before walking off.

A woman answered the door. To my surprise I saw another man and woman sitting in the room. They looked important. I didn't feel scared but I didn't know what was going on or what was about to happen.

The lady smiled at me and I felt reassured.

'Melissa, I'm Lucy and this is Peter. We are detectives from New South Wales Police. You are not in trouble. We received a phone call from your friend's mum who was worried about you because you didn't go back to school. She informed us of your situation at home. We want you to know, you don't have to go home.'

I sat down in my seat slowly and lowered my head, then burst into tears. I felt the weight of the world drop from my shoulders. Five years of carrying around what felt like a tonne on my back and my mind. On the exterior, I seemed like a happy kid but inside I felt crippled and constrained, my spirit was crushed.

I honestly thought I was living in hell. I had learned that you can't rely on anyone. In life, no-one is going to save you.

That day changed my life. I felt so much relief. I imagine it's how someone feels when they are told they are free to walk out of prison after they have been locked up for five years for a crime they didn't commit.

Having lost faith in mankind many times before I was fifteen, this day these two police officers I met restored my faith and I started to believe that maybe the world could be a good place and I wasn't living in hell.

Let me take you back a couple of weeks before this day …

It was 1984, I was twelve years old. I had just had an argument with my mum. She was reprimanding me for something I had done and yelled at me, 'You don't realise how lucky you are. You should be grateful for what you have. Your father and I adopted you to give you a better life and you are so ungrateful!'

Lucky? I thought to myself. You've got to be kidding me! I was living in hell!

In 1974, my mother and father adopted me at seventeen months. They had five children already; four boys and a girl, but they wanted another girl. They divorced when I was four. Dad re-married when I was five, but mum had a few different partners. None of them were decent. In fact they were all abusive to her, my siblings and I.

I plucked up the courage and said, 'I'm not lucky mum,' in a sombre voice. Holding back tears, she said, 'What do you mean?' I replied, 'Derek [who was her current partner] is forcing me to have sex with him.'

'Oh, so it's been you instead of me has it?'

I couldn't believe what I just heard. I was being raped! This was not consensual sex! A mother is meant to support you, believe you, and stand by you. I was beyond devastated and in a state of confusion.

She left my room and nothing more was said. I laid on my bed for the next couple of hours waiting. I didn't know what was going to happen. Mum didn't come back in to speak with me.

A few hours later my brother came past my room and said, 'Dinner.' I didn't want to go to the dining room. Not with him there. Maybe they're going to discuss it at the table with my brother present, I thought to myself.

I came to the table. 'Sit down,' my mother said in a stern voice. I sat down quietly. 'I'm not hungry,' I said. 'Eat your dinner,' my mother said sternly. I looked up to see everyone eating like it was any normal day.

My mother said, 'Derek and I have had a discussion and we have decided you are grounded for telling lies and trying to cause trouble.'

I couldn't believe my ears. My mother was not going to do anything about her partner sexually abusing me. I was in shock. I couldn't believe it was just going to be swept under the table and they expected life to keep going as normal.

Weeks later, I was picked up from school by the Department of Welfare and placed with my father and stepmother.

The detectives came to our house and asked me if I wanted to make a statement and proceed with taking my mum's boyfriend to court. Mum had two boyfriends who sexually abused me for years. They both happened to work with mum at the same workplace in Sydney.

Her first partner started abusing me on the night of my ninth birthday. Mum didn't do anything about it when I told her as she was already living with her new boyfriend, who was now abusing me. They both decided that I was too young to go to court and it was better to just forget about it and never speak of it again. Basically, just pretend it never happened.

I did make two statements and started the proceedings for a committal hearing to see if there was enough evidence to proceed with a court case. It took a lot of courage and all my strength to speak up and go through both court cases during my teenage years. The lawyers were brutal and it was humiliating retelling the incidents in graphic detail to a room full of strangers, let alone my father and stepmother.

One man was acquitted based on not enough evidence. It totally gutted me that he walked out free for the crimes he'd committed. I was robbed of my innocence.

STORIES FROM THE STREETS

The next court case resulted in a hung jury. I fought that and started a whole new committal proceeding and court case. It took three years from giving my statement until it was all over and I finally got a guilty verdict, but the sentence was only two years.

I don't regret what I did. I am proud that I fought for justice and speaking my truth. My fighting spirit wouldn't let me lay down and be treated like a piece of scum, which is how I felt for many decades after the abuse. I did it for all of the boys and girls who were also being abused and were not able to speak up and make a stand against these crimes.

Things didn't quite work out at home with my dad and stepmum for various reasons, and at fifteen I went to live with my cousin and then later my older sister, who was seventeen. She was struggling to get by herself and eventually one day she came home and said, 'I'm sorry, Lis, I lost my job. I have no money. I'm going to live with a friend. The electricity has been cut off. I've packed up everything. You just have to pack up your room.' There was no option to go back home. My dad and my stepmother had moved onto their boat.

The year was 1989. I was about to embark in my final year of high school. I felt like I had just conquered the biggest battle of my life and nothing would break me from here on in.

I packed my belongings into a green garbage bag and walked to the nearest phone booth up the street. I didn't ring my dad this time. He had paid the bond and set us up in the unit. We were both working, me at night and on the weekends to pay the rent, and food. My sister paid most of the bills. I couldn't ring him and tell him we had failed. I phoned him a few months before that and asked him for some money for a school uniform and he said he couldn't help me as he had no money. I knew I had to figure this out myself.

So I phoned the police detective I knew from my court cases and told him I had nowhere to live. He gave me the number for the Sydney City Mission.

I phoned them and they told me there was a youth refuge at Brookvale. I called and the lady at the end of the phone said, 'Yes we do have one room. When would you like to come for an interview?'

'Can I come this afternoon?' I asked. 'Yes of course,' she replied. I grabbed my green garbage bag of everything I owned, my whole life was in one garbage bag, and walked further up the street to the bus stop.

I arrived at the house. The house was a mansion, three stories high. I left my garbage bag at the front door and rang the doorbell. A lady with a big smile answered the door. 'Melissa?' 'Yes!' 'Come in.' She escorted me through the massive entrance to her office.

She explained to me that this was a youth refuge for kids who couldn't live at home. Some major sponsors had raised $1 million dollars to buy the place. There are two levels. The bottom floor with four bedrooms was for four boys, the middle floor was for four girls and the main living room, and the top floor was the kitchen and dining room, as well as where she lived with her husband and two sons.

Her husband was high up in the charity and they were also the houseparents. They had social workers there 24/7 to support the kids. She showed me around the house and explained the rules.

'There is one spare room but you will have to share with

another girl. There are house rules you need to abide by. No alcohol or drugs are to be brought onto the property and you are not to come home intoxicated or bring friends here without permission. Why don't you go home and have a think about it and then give me a call and let me know what you think.'

'There is no home. I would like to move in, please, if you'll have me. I'm a good person. I just want a safe place to complete my HSC and I need somewhere to sleep. I work hard, I have two jobs. Everything I have is at the front door in my garbage bag. I can move in now.'

I spent the next eighteen months living in the youth refuge. It was a real eye-opener. I gained so much compassion for others meeting the young kids in that refuge. It broke my heart the stories I heard. The underlying feeling we all had, was that we were not loved, not wanted and didn't belong anywhere or to anyone, that we were disposable in our families' minds. Everyone, from the fundraisers to our beautiful houseparents and the youth workers restored my faith in mankind and made me feel worthy of feeling safe and secure and I did feel loved by them.

It is not an easy job caring for youth who are really struggling mentally, but I am so grateful to them for this experience that has made me the strong woman I am today. I also completed my final year of high school and did well in my studies despite the circumstance.

Speaking up and speaking my truth got me into the situation where I found myself homeless, and then living in a youth refuge. I wouldn't change anything. In fact, I now have a career where I teach people to grow their online presence, grow their personal brand and become a recognised influencer and to use your voice and story to make a difference in the world.

My Message:
It doesn't matter where you came from or what your background is. Anyone can turn their life around and recreate themself to design a life they love. You are worthy and you matter. Today I have three children and am stepmother to another three. I have a partner who loves and respects me. I have set boundaries on how I allow people to treat me and what I will and won't tolerate. A big part of my values is contribution and I love to give back however I can. One small act of kindness can make a huge difference in someone's life and we can all do something to make a difference. Whether that is a listening ear, a shoulder to cry on, a cup of coffee, a meal, a bed, a warm blanket or clothes. We can all do something to give.

I encourage you to donate to Agape Outreach Inc. ***https://agapeoutreachinc.com*** in Tweed Heads who serve the homeless and those in need, or reach out to your local community and see where you can help.

AGAPE'S DREAM TINY HOUSING LIVING ESTATES

Where do people live when they have mental illness or physical disability preventing normal functioning and no family support? The unfortunate answer is, on the streets.

Agape Living Estates will house up to 150 chronic homeless people full-time in assisted living, offering dual diagnosis and skilled care in a respectful, self-sustaining community. On-site services will offer counselling/psychology support, visiting doctors and small wound care, as well as support groups for drug and alcohol rehabilitation and basic life skills classes.

We will promote the dignity and self-worth of all of our residents, and strive to give them excellent quality of life, as defined by the residents' individual capabilities. To that end, we will encourage participation in the upkeep of the living estate at a level relevant to the residents' capabilities. This could be cleaning bathrooms, cooking, mowing or tending to chickens or a vegetable garden.

We will provide activities that can upskill and provide group socialisation, such as cooking classes, budgeting classes, barista classes, access to a men's shed and group classes to build emotional strength.

Agape Living Estate is not just a caregiving facility, it is their home, and for those who cannot adapt back into normal community living, this will become their community and home for life.

On Agape's future five acres of land, we will build a hundred tiny houses, for permanently housing the chronic homeless. These tiny houses can house a single or couple, and twelve self-contained, two-bedroom mobile homes will house families, in a separated and fenced area. The family accommodation will be short-term residential while Agape case managers work to secure permanent housing for families. Agape Living Estate is fully supported living, including security to deal with antisocial behaviours.

We have big dreams to help many people and without support from people like you we will not be able to attain them.

Can you help us to realise this goal?

Your donation of any size will directly support the homeless with accommodation, food and needs that are their basic human rights.

Agape Outreach Inc. is DGR registered, meaning that we are a tax deductible registered charity. Any donation $2 and above is tax deductible, and greatly appreciated.

Some ideas of what your money can support with Agape are:
- $1.80 provides a nutritious meal for a homeless person,
- $39 provides a care pack with backpack, tarp, insect spray, blanket and sunscreen,
- $100 provides seventeen tarps to help keep people and their belongings dry,
- $570 puts a vulnerable person into a motel for a week,
- $1260 will feed Agape's clients for a week,
- $18,000 will buy a tiny house for the Tiny Housing Living Estate,

STORIES FROM THE STREETS

- $35,000 provides money to set up a rental house for six or more people.

The cost of land is Agape's biggest challenge, with high costs that change day to day, as land that is zoned for residential development is in high demand. If anyone is in a position to donate towards land or has land to donate with the appropriate zoning, it would help so many people.

Direct deposits can be made into Agape's bank account, please contact Agape for the bank details on ***0414 693 670*** and donations can also be made through Agape's website ***www.agapeoutreachinc.com***

THERESA MITCHELL

Working on the 'fringe' is Theresa's heart and specialty. Her passion for encouraging people for life shines through daily, whether from the stage presenting, or to supporting homeless people on the streets.

In 2009, Theresa founded, and is currently the director, of Agape Outreach Inc. - a charity supporting the homeless and needy with food, psychology access, case management and basic life skill classes.

She is the author of *Stories from the Streets*. Theresa has opened her own psychology department to aid the homeless and is also completing her own clinical psychology degree to be able to personally help more people holistically. Theresa's desire and aim is to open the tiny housing living estates for the homeless and then duplicate the Agape model of support for the homeless from street outreach to housing around Australia.

In 2015, Theresa was named Woman of the Year in Tweed Shire for inspiring so many in the community and has been recognised in many community service awards since. She was a finalist in the Hesta Community Hero Awards, a finalist four times in the NSW Woman of the Year state awards, and won the Australia Day Volunteer of the Year award for Tweed Shire in 2019.

STORIES FROM THE STREETS

Her speaking is a rare combination of being able to pull out your passions and being able to inspire you to live them today. Theresa can be contacted via the Agape website: ***www.agape-outreachinc.com*** or email: ***admin@agapeoutreachinc.com***

www.ingramcontent.com/pod-product-compliance
Lightning Source LLC
Chambersburg PA
CBHW031254290426
44109CB00012B/575